T0103649

Inspiration in Small Doses

Uplifting Short Stories and Essays

MICHELE K. SYNEGAL

abbott press

Abbott Press books may be ordered through booksellers or by contacting:

Abbott Press
1663 Liberty Drive
Bloomington, IN 47403
www.abbottpress.com
Phone: 1 (866) 697-5310

ISBN: 978-1-4582-1930-5 (sc)
ISBN: 978-1-4582-1931-2 (hc)
ISBN: 978-1-4582-1932-9 (e)

Library of Congress Control Number: 2015912655

Print information available on the last page.

Abbott Press rev. date: 02/09/2016

TABLE OF CONTENTS

Dedication

I dedicate this book in memory of my parents Betty Jean Little and James Synegal, who now sleep with the angels.

Acknowledgements

For many years, this book languished as merely an idea and topic of conversation at social gatherings. But it came to fruition because of the support and encouragement of my family and friends. I am, therefore, grateful to Briana and Sharif Mitchell, my children, for allowing me to broadcast some of our experiences. I am thankful to my mother, Betty Little, for verifying the accuracy of my distant memory. I wish to thank Gary Klinga, Karen James Cody and Auset Lee Lewis for editing, organizing, and enhancing my work. I am indebted to Jocelyn Wolfe for providing an international distribution outlet. Many thanks to Robin Jantay in India, who created the book cover design idea while I slept nights in America, as he worked diligently to have designs for me to review by morning.

My deepest and sincerest gratitude goes to Ernest Holmes, who I frequently quoted in the book. He is the founder of Religious Science, a practical philosophy by which I live and to which I have dedicated my life. His teachings helped me discover my life's work and my soul's purpose.

To my family at Spiritual Empowerment Center, especially those in the Power of Your Word classes, DeBora Ricks, and the Writer's Support Group, I am humbly grateful for your love and support. All are a source of inspiration to me. A million times, I thank you.

Introduction

This book is an offering to help you find those elusive keys that unlock the doors to richer living. I convey ideas by first telling my stories because stories can be powerful tools. Stories activate not only the language parts of our brain but the whole brain. When we hear a story we want to relate it to one of our existing experiences. My stories are intended to inspire, educate, challenge, captivate, and make emotional connections to help you the reader, better understand the message that is therein, for you. The stories I tell are the stories that I have lived and if I am successful, help you relate to similar experiences of pain, joy, enlightenment or else.

And from scores of talks I delivered to my congregation over a period of several years, I have produced a collection of essays. I develop and address topics in the form of sermons focused on ageless subjects for a month, allowing both me and the congregation time to explore the topic at depth. My hope is that where needed, you will be motivated to bring about changes in your life inspired by the information provided in the essays.

I too had been searching for a life filled with meaning and purpose. My expedition led me across the globe to different churches, temples, religions, philosophies and even a flirtation with the paranormal. My orientation is not theological but rather spiritual and practical in its outlook.

I have traveled for more than forty years and learned many lessons about truth, myself and God and that there is so much more to life than things, material. I have contemplated the faculties and qualities of the Divine and endeavor to possess those qualities; through my journey I found the keys that open the doors to love, peace, joy, happiness and fulfillment.

Ultimately, I pray that this book offers you a new way of examining life, expanding your awareness, and delivering fresh insight into the big questions about our existence. I further hope that it provides the guidance you need to find your own most meaningful place in life's universal story.

The stories are my distant memories which have faded a bit over the years.

To protect the privacy of others, names have been changed and some characters conflated.

Part I

WORK, MONEY & SUCCESS

Cyber Job Search

"Toto, I've a feeling we're not in Kansas anymore." That memorable line spoken by Dorothy in the film *The Wizard of Oz* is a poignant metaphor for "Things have drastically changed." Over the past few years it hasn't been business as usual for my company, so I realized that I had to change if I expected to eat on a regular basis. After more than twenty years of owning a business and enjoying robust profitability, I was faced with a difficult choice: to either generate new business in a "down economy" or seek gainful employment in a "growth industry." I chose the latter.

I hadn't applied for employment since 1982, and things are done so differently now. I met with a career consultant to narrow down my search before I actually began looking for employment. I had to become a savvy job seeker in the age of online job boards, video résumés, virtual interviews, social networking, and the least personal of all—preliminary interviews via Instant Messaging!

I paid to have my résumé written so that the proper keywords were selected for scanning, and so that it would advance beyond the first gatekeeper. Nowadays, your electronic résumé must be "camera ready" and able to be scanned. I paid a digital marketing service – BeFound – to bring me into the electronic age. BeFound showed me how to establish my online presence on LinkedIn and Google, and showcase my skill sets by including a "word cloud" that characterized my strengths and expertise. Did I mention that my résumé had to be strategically positioned for optimization too? That means that recruiters can just Google a phrase, such as "learning and development." All persons with a correctly worded, scanned, and optimized résumé will "be found." And most certainly, each job seeker wants theirs to pop up at the top of the listing, which requires strategic positioning.

I must admit that initially I was frustrated. Each organization's online application required that I set up a profile, and if I applied for multiple jobs within that company, I had better be sure that I clicked on the résumé that matched that particular job. I blew it once and was thought to be "technologically incompetent." Ouch! Each time I applied for a position I spent hours tailoring my résumé and cover letter so that my applicable experience was emphasized. Finding a full-time job literally became my full-time job!

When I was not selected, I was lucky if I received an email letting me know. Most companies don't even respond these days, whether by email, voice mail, or "snail mail." It was as though my applications dropped into a bottomless abyss, never to surface again.

The truth of the matter, as it turns out, is that even in this new age of cyber employment seeking, getting an interview, I suspected, would come down to the old school way of "knowing someone on the inside." The interviews granted to me all came because I had a friend in a senior position within a company. Through their introductions my résumé received special consideration. Thus, after a great deal of fruitless work, my suspicion was confirmed that the old "who you know" game still plays a key role in the employment process.

As the months passed by I had to remain faith-filled, optimistic, and prayed up! My spiritual practices of affirmative prayer, visualization, positive affirmations, and the power of intention kept me in the game. I came across the positive affirmation that Aibileen Clark (the maid in the movie *The Help*) used to say to Mae Mobley (the little girl she cared for): "You is pretty. You is smart. You is important!" I laugh every time I recite it to myself. Humor was my elixir.

Staying away from the doomsayers was extremely important too. God bless them, but their apocalyptic visions about my future were just too depressing, especially 'Doubting Thomas.' He implored me to be more realistic and less the dreamer. He strongly suggested that I think about the worst-case scenarios that could result in homelessness and dire poverty. And from that mindset I was advised to develop a Plan B. Yikes! That consciousness, I reckoned, would attract those much-undesired results to my experience. No thank you! Singing, dancing, playing tennis, and listening to upbeat music gave me the lift in consciousness I needed to press forward.

There are, however, some advantages to cyber job search. You can apply to tens of jobs in one day, and the rejection emails may or may not come. Because the recruitment process is extremely impersonal, it's easier not to take the rejection and denials personally.

My point: until you land your ideal job or the realization of a goal, keep asking, keep searching, and keep knocking. That right and perfect opportunity will find its way to you! Though knowing someone on the inside got me interviews, I was eventually found on LinkedIn and hired as a contractor with a few companies, simultaneously. All of my long suffering finally paid off.

Affirmation

Every negative thought or condition is erased from my experience. I walk in the joy of expectancy of ever-increasing good in the form of right income-generating opportunities as I press forward. I accept my good right now.

Money: The Big, Scary Ogre

There is little likelihood that your life can become fully functioning with prosperity, unless you have a positive and creative attitude toward money.
ERIC BUTTERWORTH

For over thirty years I have facilitated tens of personal development courses. And in all those years, the one thing that most people seem to fear most is money. Though what they have in common are their fears about money, their issues span a broad spectrum: the fear of not having enough, the fear of having too much, the fear of misusing it, the fear of losing it, and the mother lode of fears—the fear of not being worthy to receive it in significant amounts.

Money is a big, scary ogre to many people, though in and of itself it is just a means of exchange and a currency of divine flow. The fear of it has grown in gargantuan, frightening proportions because some people actually define themselves in terms of how much or how little money they have. Their self-worth and self-esteem are often intricately intertwined with their finances.

Consciousness alone determines the amount of money that flows in and out of our lives. Before we can experience financial success in the world, we must first see ourselves as financially successful in our minds. Poverty and wealth are both states of mind. The first thing we must do to keep the scary ogre at bay is to change our thinking about money. Our attitude toward it either attracts more of it to us or repels it. When we feel deserving of it, even entitled to it, then it comes. When we appreciate what money we do have and give thanks for it, then more will come. When we are steadfast in our faith that our every need will always be supplied, then more comes.

A consciousness of prosperity can be developed with time and attention. First you must start thinking about your money and your finances in a positive and confident way. If you practice this long enough it will become a habit, and eventually the natural way in which you think. Think about and visualize what being financially free would look and feel like. Next, develop your attitude of positive expectation and gratitude, both of which are energetic forces that draw to you that which you conceive in your mind.

Having a positive attitude and relationship with money is one aspect of developing wealth. The other is acting on ideas. Ideas too are currency. In his timeless classic, *Spiritual Economics*, Eric Butterworth said: "we are always only one idea away from wealth." Ideas come to us all the time. Converting those ideas into money-making ventures requires action. Acting on even a small idea develops our skills and builds our confidence to implement plans that bring our ideas into reality.

I got an idea that the spiritual organization in which I am involved could increase its visibility through service to the communities where our centers are based. I presented the idea to the senior leadership, who accepted my plan for a "World Day of Service." I wrote a guide to developing community service projects, and our communications department established a media marketing campaign. A logo was designed and we branded print materials.

The organization didn't pay me for my idea, but the idea did become a money generating enterprise for me. I was later hired by a financial services company to establish and implement their community service program because of my enthusiasm and excitement about ours.

Don't be fearful of money or be in denial about your finances. Grow your prosperity consciousness to the point whereby you can separate yourself from your finances. You are not your money! Face your financial challenges with a positive attitude knowing that they didn't come to stay; they, like everything else, came to pass. Take time to think and allow ideas to come to you that might just be the solution to your financial adversity or may lead to a profitable venture.

Affirmation

Money and prosperity come to me through my consciousness of abundance. I do not allow fear and feelings of unworthiness to occupy space in my mind. I confidently remain open to the flow of ideas and I create new realities by acting on these ideas. I am grateful for the unlimited possibilities of the Divine, flowing as money and prosperity into my life now.

Swiss Alps Look Out! Here I Come!

Persistent people begin their success where others end in failure.
EDWARD EGGLESTON

"I'm an athlete. I can do this!" This is what I told myself the entire week as I took last place at the end of every ski run. When I agreed with my husband, Thomas, and a group of our closest friends that we needed a winter sport, we chose skiing. I was then oblivious to the fact that physical fitness is a requirement. Don't the skis do all the work?

Our first ski adventure took place only a few months after I gave birth to my first child, Sharif. I was thirty pounds over my pre-pregnancy weight and hadn't seen the inside of a gym for over a year. I was adjusting to motherhood and holding down a full-time job. I had started playing tennis again six weeks after delivery, but it wasn't enough to get me in real shape for walking in boots that had to weigh at least five pounds each with five-foot, weighted sticks strapped to them. At first, I was so clumsy that I stumbled over the tips of my skis and fell down just trying to stand still. But my excitement and enthusiasm were never lost. I am competitive by nature, so didn't let my failed attempts at skiing get the best of me.

After this first ski trip I decided to consult my dear friend, Katie, who grew up in Racine, Wisconsin, and had skied many weekends during their very long, cold winters. Once I visited her in January when the temperature was 9° below zero; my teeth chatter at the memory. Discreetly, I approached her about teaching me to ski. I wanted private lessons without the pressure of being teased for being the last one down the mountain—again. She kindly agreed.

Lake Tahoe was about three and a half hours away from my home in Oakland, California. We chose Alpine Meadows, one of Lake Tahoe's winter resorts, so one morning about 4:00 a.m. Katie and I loaded up my van and headed north for a ski adventure. On the drive up we talked about technique and safety precautions. She asked me to visualize coming down the mountain in full control, wind at my back and a smile on my face. I had designer suits and custom boots, so I knew that my appearance was impeccable. I just needed the ability to make those outfits the object of onlookers' attention, rather than the sight of my body sprawled horizontally on the snow covered mountain.

Having managed to graduate from the 'wedge method,' and then able to get on and off the lift chair without mishaps, with Katie's guidance I started skiing on the blue runs which are designed for intermediate level skiers. Katie was very patient and constantly encouraged me to relax and enjoy the experience. We went up and down the same run a half dozen times before I was totally confident and at ease. At the start of the seventh run I was mentally psyched to race her. Of course she beat me, but I was only a couple of minutes behind. I knew that if I could stay on my feet and match her speed, I would dust the others the next time we all went skiing.

I had a six-month-old baby at home, so we had to drive back the same day. During the ride back Katie asked me if I remembered Scott Ridge. I remembered it vividly because I didn't actually ski down the first time we met. I took my skis off and clumsily walked down, because I was too scared of the steep decline. When I stood at the top of that run (elevation at 8,289 feet) and looked down, I became paralyzed. There was no way I was going down that mountain on skis. She then informed me that our last run of the day had been, in fact, Scott Ridge. I was amazed. I hadn't even realized it. By that time, I was so relaxed and confident that I'd just followed her down the mountain. I was no longer paying attention to which run we were on. I was exuberant! In my zealousness I declared, "Swiss Alps look out. Here I come!"

Two years and ten private ski lessons later, Thomas and I went skiing in Zermatt, Switzerland, a winter wonderland. We were chauffeured to the ski runs by horse-drawn sleighs. The snow was in naturally perfect condition. At the end of the day hot chocolate awaited us at the lodge. That was one of the best experiences of my life, making all those early morning and late night drives back and forth between Oakland and Lake Tahoe well worth it.

Some of my friends quit after the first experience. They will never know the pleasure of riding high in the sky and taking in the beauty of the snow covered mountains, clear blue skies, or of sharing hot chocolate in front of the fireplace with loved ones at the end of a perfect ski day. Some people begin their success where others end in failure.

Affirmation

Success is mine! Failure is not an option. I persistently pursue my goals and dreams until they are realized. The doorway of my consciousness has the word **SUCCESS** *written boldly above it. I am confident in my ability to succeed in all I attempt with earnest desire.*

Part II

PERSEVERANCE

When Drowning in Two Feet
of Water, Just Stand!

*What do you do when you've done all you can
and it seems like you can't make it through?
What do you do when there is nothing left to do?
Child, you just stand!*
DONNIE MCCLURKIN

I had a near-death experience at about age six. It happened one day when I went fishing with one of my mother's suitors, Jerry. Our little fishing boat capsized in a lake in Southern California. I didn't know how to swim because my mother feared the water and rarely took us to the beach, though we lived in Los Angeles, just a short distance from all the California beaches that stretch from Santa Monica to Manhattan. I had inherited that same fear, so, unable to swim; I panicked when I fell in the lake. I did everything that could have led to my demise—flailing arms, bobbing up then back down below the surface, and in the process swallowing more of the lake water each time I went under. Jerry saved me by swimming over and pulling me out, finally getting me back inside the boat. Now that I think back, it was really a small canoe; but at six years old everything seemed so big. We were on the Titanic, weren't we?

Fast forward thirty-five years to a time when I almost drowned again; one frightening day while frolicking with my children in the Raging Waters at Disney World. My children know how to swim because I made certain they learned. Sharif was nine and Briana seven when we partook of all the thrilling rides and water activities that Orlando had to offer. My children loved to play in water. Whether it was swimming, white water rafting, or running and jumping onto the "Slip and Slide" in our backyard, they loved water. They were in Olympic-sized swimming pools before they could walk across a room without falling. I didn't want them growing up with that ominous fear of death by drowning like I had.

When they begged and pleaded to play in the Raging Waters—much to my chagrin—I obliged. It was fun splashing in the cool water on a 100° F day with 95 per cent humidity. Thirty or so minutes into my 'hydro-massage' the flood gates opened. I hadn't known that there was any significance to the name of the play area—Raging Waters. I found out quickly, though, when the force of the waves knocked me down. I opened my eyes as wide as saucers and flailed my arms to keep my head above the waves. But the water continued to rush out with great force, and my attempts to keep my head above water seemed to be increasingly in vain.

Sharif yelled to the lifeguard: "Save my mom; she's drowning!" The lifeguard yelled from his director's chair, "Just stand!" In my panicked state, my mind couldn't comprehend what he was saying. I was too busy fighting for my life. In a flash the lifeguard got off his chair and lifted me out of the water until I was standing. When I finally calmed down and regained my composure, I looked down to see that I was, in fact, standing in about two feet of water.

My near-death experience symbolizes a great metaphor for the struggles that we allow to drown us. They seem humongous while we are going through them, but once we have processed and worked through them they often appear small and shallow. Instead of panicking and flailing in our troubles, we simply need to stand! Stand still. Collect our wits. Breathe deeply. Relax and access the ever available reservoir of resources we have within us.

Drowning is believed to be one of the worst kinds of death to suffer. It's painful and disempowering. Drowning in our problems feels much the same way—painful and disempowering. Yet, there is an alternative: just stand. Stand in the experience, meeting it head on. Stand on truth and principle, knowing that on the other side there is peace. To get to the other side you must first grow through the experience. Stand in knowing that these waves too shall recede. When you stop and face your troubles, the likelihood is great that you'll realize that they, like the water at Raging

Waters, are only about two feet deep—and your best course of action is to stand. Stand up to them and be fully present to what you are thinking and feeling. Then let the living waters of Spirit bathe, guide, and heal you.

Affirmation

I do not drown in my problems. They have no power over me. I face them head on. I allow myself to feel whatever emotions rise to the surface. And when I have done all that I can do, I just stand and let the living waters of Spirit guide, nurture, and heal me.

From Cleaning Rags to Riches

The vision that you glorify in your mind, the ideal that you enthrone in your heart, this you will build your life by and this you will become.
JAMES ALLEN

My grandmother and I were discussing my plans for the future when I blurted out with arrogance, "I don't want to be anybody's maid. There will be no cleaning of other people's toilets for me!" Without warning, she smacked the side of my face with her hand. "Housekeeping is good, honest work!" she shouted. Grandmother Josephine then reminded me that cleaning other folks' toilets had paid for piano lessons, the theater, the Ice Capades, and all of the other wonderful experiences she provided me and my sisters as children growing up in the City of Angels, close to Hollywood, home to the rich and famous.

I hadn't meant any disrespect; I just aspired to be more. I knew that with access to education I would be able to run a company or rise to the executive suite of a major corporation. I had plans—big plans—that didn't include being a domestic. My plans were to go to college then find a "good" job. It was also my goal to become a master of my craft and eventually work for myself. I was determined to be the first successful business owner in my family. I was one of the first in my family to graduate from college, then one of the first to earn a master's degree. God gifted me with a good mind, and like the NAACP commercials used to say, "A mind is a terrible thing to waste." I couldn't imagine wasting mine mopping the floors of Mr. T, the movie director who employed my grandmother.

I worked hard in school to get excellent grades to be eligible for scholarships. I applied myself daily so that I could gain admission to the schools of my choice. And I did just that! Though my writing wasn't the best in those days, my reading comprehension and verbal communication skills were excellent. My cousin Melvin always said that I should be a politician because I definitely had the gift of gab. I talked my way into a full scholarship the first year.

Yet, although I had a college education, an advanced degree even, and would earn hundreds of thousands more than my grandmother ever had, she was a woman who always made the most of what she had, and she lived a life that many envied. She was on the deaconess board of her church, was a founding member of the Women's Sunday Morning Breakfast Club, and became First Lady of Neighborhood Community Church when she married its new, hotshot preacher from Indianapolis while in her seventies, I might add.

As I reflect on her life, I must acknowledge that my grandmother was an amazing woman. She learned a great deal from observing what her employers did to attain prosperity, and invested in the same stocks and bonds. She even learned to play golf like they did. Every year she traveled on real vacations to distant places I had only dreamed of, like Hawaii and London. She owned her own home and had income property to boot. She did well for herself, and today is still my role model. She was deeply spiritual, and this is something else I learned from her and which is a part of her legacy to me.

Grandmother never gave up on her vision of living an exalted life or relinquished the ideals that enthroned her heart. She always walked with her head held high, wore the finest clothes, spoke with confidence, and stayed in prayer. Today I am humble and wise enough to appreciate her accomplishments. Though she may have started out cleaning toilets, she later paid other domestics to clean hers, always treating them with the utmost dignity and respect.

The moral of this story is that regardless of where you start off in life you can rise above your circumstances to live a glorified life. Like my grandmother, make the most of what you have. Do whatever it is you do with excellence. Watch, learn, and apply the knowledge you possess to the betterment of your life and the life of others.

Affirmation

I embody the vision in my mind of having a wonderful life. My idea of my perfect life is enthroned in my heart. I imagine it. I breathe it. I make the most of what I have, applying what I know, to live the life of my dreams.

Holy Matrimony

I will dwell in the house of the Lord forever.
PSALM 23:6

I recently witnessed the marriage of one of my son's best friends, Brandon, to a lovely girl, Monica. As I reflect on the ceremony, I realize that the wedding held a deeper meaning for me, more so than just witnessing public vows and partaking of festivities.

I saw the coming together of two diverse cultures—Filipino and African-American. At the wedding we consumed food from the Philippines and danced to the soulful R&B hits of the '70s, '80s, and '90s. I witnessed the union of the universal masculine with the universal feminine: the strong, disciplined determination of personal will, and the soft and gentle strength of obedience to God's Will. Both partners possess each of these qualities though they manifest differently as their unique personalities. God's Will and our personal will are interdependent if we live spiritually and must coexist if our individual human potential, and the potentiality of Brandon and Monica's union, are to be fulfilled.

After the marriage vows were exchanged and the pronouncement made that "they are now married in the eyes of God" in the great state of Texas before their families and friends, they started their married life together by receiving Holy Communion. In doing so, they honored the recognition of God's place in their lives and in their marriage, uniting the human with the divine.

It is true that in order for each of us to fulfill the potentiality of our being, if each of us is to be self-actualized, then we too must develop a strong and determined will to succeed while maintaining an awareness of and honoring the Presence of God's Will for our lives. As you read these words you might be thinking that you do not know God's Will for your life. Or you might be asking, *How does anyone ever really know what the Divine Plan is, and what my role in it is?*

Developing an ongoing communion with the Divine that dwells within is a good place to start. Guidance and clarity come from within, expressing as hunches or desires, intuition or epistemology—knowing things beyond our human comprehension with a profound sense of confidence, yet not knowing from whence this knowing comes. What I realize is that when I am determined to do something that is for the highest good of all concerned and from that I cannot be deterred, I am supported by the Universe, and all conspires to produce my heart's desire.

For instance, when I married God during my ordination, which was the public acceptance of my vows to honor and serve the Almighty by ministering to humanity for the rest of my life, I was fully supported from on High. I believed that if I held the vision of what I dreamed my ordination to be, and the vision was strong and compelling, God would make all the necessary provisions.

I said "Yes" to what I then thought was a random invitation to participate in a panel discussion at the University of Baltimore, in their newly constructed Student Center, home to the Wright Theater. Sitting on that stage we were encouraged to listen to a musical composition written and performed by Robert Hitz, an accomplished local pianist. He asked us to let the music transport us to wherever it did while fully embodying the experience and engaging all of our senses.

I was transported to a vision of my ordination ceremony taking place on that very stage – a state-of-the art auditorium which was large enough and regal enough to accommodate all of my family and friends. I imagined myself on that stage receiving the white, linen and gold lamè stole that adorns the shoulders of ordained ministers of our order. I dreamed of beautiful, fragrant flowers serving as bookends on both sides of the stage. My mouth watered in anticipation of partaking of savory dishes prepared with elegance and flair. I reveled in the music of an accomplished, gifted pianist and angelic voices as they expressed my feelings in song.

I held that vision of opulence and beauty while fully recognizing the financial reality that the cost to rent the theater was way more than my church had budgeted for a venue. But, I still held the vision that my ordination ceremony would take place at that very theater.

Through much prayer, visualization and creativity, my dream came true. I realized that there are many ways to accomplish what we set our hearts on. When we stay in close communion with God, the far-fetched becomes reachable.

I resolved the matter by bartering with the university, offering my time and expertise as a lecturer on three occasions in lieu of the rental fee. I met a florist who donated his services to select and arrange flowers that I purchased at wholesale prices. My church's music ministry performed my favorite songs with grace and splendor as their gift to me. I met a wonderful chef who prepared succulent delights at a cost we could afford.

When God is first in our lives, it is His pleasure to give us the Kingdom—the desires of our hearts. I liken my relationship with God to Brandon and Monica's marriage: they each married their best friend and placed God at the center. I too committed my life to my best friend and surrendered my will to His Will, placing God at the very center of my being.

Therefore, place God at the center of all you do and watch the windows of heaven open and pour out blessings which you will hardly be able to contain.

Affirmation

God is all there is. I unify with all that God is. I dedicate my life to developing an intimate relationship with Spirit. I accept all of my blessings. And so it is.

Part III

CHANGE

Seasons of Change

Summer ends, and autumn comes, and he who would have it otherwise would have high tide always and a full moon every night.
HAL BORLAND

The summer of living in my beautiful and spacious home was ending. And like the last leaves of autumn, clinging desperately to the branches, I had been clinging to the wonderful memories of yesteryear. "My children grew up in this house," is what I said to myself in finding justification for staying longer. "But really, it just doesn't make sense anymore," the cobwebs in the empty rooms cried out in protest to my staying.

We celebrated so many wonderful milestones in this house – my daughter's cotillion, high school and college graduations; my son's rite of passage into manhood; and my own journey into ministry with all its pomp and circumstance. I usually welcome change; in fact I thrive on it, but it was different this time. Why? Was it because I didn't know where I'd go if I moved? Or was it because suburban living had become what I came to know so well? Or was it because it's where my new life began after the passing of my husband? It's probably for all those reasons, and if I liken this situation to the changing of the seasons, I know that every year summer indeed does end and autumn does come. If it were otherwise, I would have high tides always and full moons every night. What I mean is that I would only keep on knowing what I already know. I would stifle my own growth and limit unforeseen possibilities.

Just like nature knows when it's time to change seasons, I too knew it was time to move out and to move on. Speaking of seasons, the great thing about winter is that it provides much time for reflection and anticipation. The long nights are perfect for being still and imagining what might be, while spring promises new life. By changing my thoughts about moving, I changed my perspective and, subsequently, opened my mind to new possibilities.

After surviving all of the 'firsts' without my husband, that is, the first Thanksgiving, the first Christmas, and the first New Year's Eve, I vowed to create new traditions so that my children and I would have fresh memories. Creating newness for my family meant moving to a new location, building a colonial house that was a big departure from our Californian and Floridian ultramodern homes, starting new schools, and hanging my shingle over a new office door. Our lives did change. Instead of mourning our loss during winter vacations at Lake Tahoe, we traveled to New York City to the theatre and the Christmas Show at Radio City Music Hall. We summered on Martha's Vineyard, which became our east coast vacation paradise. Even today it's my son's favorite place to unwind and spend time with friends.

Instead of living life in retrospect, I can design a brand new life anytime. And so can you! Andre Gide wrote, "Man cannot discover new oceans unless he has the courage to lose sight of the shore." If you want to have new and different experiences, then leave the shore of what you already know. Have the courage to set your intention on the life that you desire. Where you place your attention creates a new pattern of experience, possibility, and opportunity.

I did finally move and felt liberated after doing so. I now look forward to new oceans, the shores of the unfamiliar, decorating many new homes, meeting new neighbors, and starting more new family traditions.

Affirmation

There is a time for everything, and a season for every activity under the heavens.
Ecclesiastes 3:1

Forever Changed

Change is the only cosmological constant.
AMY TAN

We are the sum total of all of our experiences, are we not? I believe this and believe that our lives can be forever changed by one pivotal moment in time. Mine was November 16, 1994 about 2:30 p.m.

I was on the telephone in my home office in Miami, discussing a major project with my client at HBO. We talked for an hour, with both of us volleying questions and answers back and forth, determining all probable scenarios and their solutions before the launch of our company-wide, online survey.

Back then fax machines were in heavy use, and with mine each page sounded as though it were being typed on my first manual Corona – the kind where you can hear each keystroke, like the telegraph machines in classic Westerns. By page five I started to become annoyed by that sound. I thought, "That sure is a long fax. Is it ever going to end?" Page ten dropped to the floor when the tray overflowed. I ended my conversation and ran over to see what in God's name was being transmitted and by whom.

Thomas had stayed behind in Oakland to serve as on-site project manager of a lucrative contract with Lawrence Livermore Laboratory that our firm had just been awarded. The kids and I relocated to Miami according to plan so that they could start school at the beginning of the semester. Being the "new kids" was stressful enough, so we were mindful of not adding more stress by having them start mid-year when the contract with the laboratory ended.

We had just returned from the Doral Country Club having celebrated my fortieth birthday two days before the fax, so I never imagined that it was Thomas who might be sending it.

The last page of the fax was handwritten in my husband's doctor-like scrawl: "You will find my body in the storage room."

My mouth flew open as I started praying out loud, "No, God. Oh, please don't let this be happening!"

I called Thomas but he didn't answer. My mind raced a hundred miles a minute. I dialed two of my friends who lived near our family home in Oakland. Santa was reluctant to go but agreed to do so if Edward would meet her there. Edward felt obligated to go because he knew that the gun that Thomas might use to end his life belonged to him. I myself had taken it away from Edward when he was in a fit of rage after discovering his wife's infidelity. Thomas had put it away for safekeeping.

I was on the other end of the phone and I could hear Edward and Santa pounding on the door and calling Thomas' name. "There he is!" Edward shouted. He pleaded with Thomas, who was peeking out from behind the curtain, to please let him in. Thomas closed the curtain with a swift move and a deranged look in his eyes. His carefully laid plans were being interrupted.

At the pace of a machine gun shooting hundreds of rounds a minute, I shouted instructions to Edward on where to find the spare key. He ran to the old brick chimney out back, reached in, and grabbed it. He sprinted to the front door. As he slid the key into the lock, we all heard the one shot, and I heard the drone of the dial tone as a shocked Edward unknowingly broke the connection.

On the long, painful flight to California I had much time to think. With one gunshot, life as I knew it was over. In a flash, Michele, Thomas' wife of thirteen years became Michele, the forty-year-old, widowed mother of two.

My first thoughts were of my children and how they might react to the loss of their father. I wondered how I would tell them. I thought a lot about being a single parent and having to raise a male child in a new city where I felt I had no real support base. I wondered if I was capable of generating the kind of income necessary to maintain our current lifestyle. I wondered if loneliness would be a constant companion. I wondered if I would be a black widow for the rest of my life. I thought about so many things.

Though I lived through the tragic ending of my husband's life and our marriage, I had the chance to begin anew. I became the architect of my future which didn't come without effort. Once I was able to control my grief, I began to think about all the things that I had longed to do, things of which Thomas had no interest, like living on the east coast, for one.

One Saturday, the kids and I mounted a large map on the wall in my home office. Next we stuck red push pins in the cities we thought we might want to live. Then we visited those cities over a two year period and in some cases multiple times. By consensus we decided upon the Washington, D.C. area.

On one of our visits to Silver Spring, Maryland, my God-son Gibran, introduced us to a golf course community north and east of downtown Washington. We had a house built in Hampshire Greens, and began again, leaving the tragedy and humiliation of Thomas' suicide behind in Miami.

I became the designer of my future by employing all the lessons that I am sharing in this book. Adapting to change is the main one here. I adapted to a major change of which I had no control. Instead of allowing it to devastate me, I chose to see the opportunities it provided. I had the chance to live in another part of the country. I had the chance to raise my children exactly as I pleased. I never thought that I would be widowed at such a young age or a single-parent, but I was, so I made the most of my new found status.

My daily spiritual practices of prayer and meditation were the tools I used to rise above the tragedy of losing Thomas. Reading inspirational books and listening to uplifting music kept me motivated to continue to pursue my dreams. My children in their resiliency inspired me beyond measure.

What I want you take away from this story is that change is constant, and we don't get to plan all of the changes that life serves up. What we do get to do is choose how we will respond to them. My advice to you is, to see the opportunities that change presents and then seize them.

Affirmation:

Today, I declare that I get to choose how I respond to change. I proclaim that life is an eternal adventure of different experiences and I am grateful for them all.

Part IV

GRATITUDE

Gratitude: Be Thankful for Your God-given Gifts and Talents

There are two kinds of talent, a man-made talent and God-given talent.
With man-made talent you have to work very hard.
With God-given talent, you just touch it up once in a while.
PEARL BAILEY

Be thankful for your God-given gifts and talents. One way of expressing gratitude for your gifts and talents is to use them, that is to express them, and by doing so, give them to the world.

A couple of years ago I screened a movie called *The Black Tulip*. I was so moved by the movie that I haven't stopped thinking about it. After 9/11, Sonia Nassery Cole, an Afghan-American writer, filmmaker and social activist, wrote *The Black Tulip* based on the true story of an Afghan family. She made the film to portray the truth as she knows it about the Afghan people because their image has been tarnished by the terrorist acts of the Taliban and Al Qaida.

Sonia decided that the only way to express her God-given talents and to provide another perspective on Muslims was to make a film. Such an expression was no easy feat because she wanted to film it in war-torn Afghanistan. The plot was simple: after 2011, when the Taliban was at its height, an Afghan family opened the Poet's Corner, a restaurant, with an open microphone, inviting everyone to read poetry, perform music, and tell their stories. The Taliban vehemently denounced such goings on, and so the family's new-found hope in a war-torn country proved fleeting as it struggled to maintain the restaurant and vibrant, unrepressed way of life.

Sonia was born and raised in Afghanistan to parents who were part of the literary and intellectual society of the country. The family fled the country in 1979, relocating to the United States. After 9/11 she wanted to tell the world that the Taliban are not true to the Islamic faith and that the Afghan people are, in fact, peaceful, God-loving people. For the film to be authentic she felt compelled to film on location in Kabul.

The odds were against her from the very beginning when she insisted that she film inside an active war zone. The Taliban fiercely opposed the film and did everything they could to halt its production, including, extortion, attempted kidnapping, and death threats.

I will share two parts in the story that I think best illustrate *spiritual resiliency,* a powerful inner quality. Sonia went to have her hair dyed in preparation for her role in the film. At the salon, she posed a poignant question to her stylist Tammim: "How do you manage to stay so jolly amidst the death, destruction and daily bombings?"

Tammim said, "Oh Sonia Jan, if not laughing and joking, what should one do? From the day I was born, I have lived under the bomb and the shadow of death. I never know if I will make it through the day. I have lost so many of my friends. So I live every day as if it was my last. I think in life I have two choices: to live miserably every day or to live happily. I have chosen to live happily, to look at the gift that God has given me, and to live every day to the fullest. Who knows what will happen in the next moment?"

There is great wisdom in Tammim's words—live life to the fullest in the "eternal now" moment. Now is what we have. And the truth of the matter is that tomorrow isn't promised to us and we can do nothing about the past other than change our perspective about what happened.

On the fifth day of production, the first free Afghan election was held. This was a dangerous time. The Taliban did everything they could to stop the elections—suicide bombings, rocket attacks, and torture, all employed to interrupt the voting process. The media continuously issued warnings for people to exercise safety and caution. In fear for their lives, Sonia's American production crew held a covert meeting without her, to plan their departure. They all said that she could die for her faith, but they weren't ready to commit their lives to her cause, albeit, noble.

Sonia told them that she would stay and do anything and everything to complete the film. She had risked everything in her life to tell this story about the hearts and the spirit of Afghan people, her people. Her story is a story about perseverance. So how could she give up? She admitted that life was in and of itself a challenge, but she would not leave Afganistan. "This is a test of truth," she said. "I will find a way to finish the film." She later told them that it is strange that, just when one feels like falling apart in the abyss of emotional distress, as was the case with Sonia, there comes the sweetest feeling of awakening to one's personal power. When we are in distress, what there is to do is to pray to God to give us the strength to persevere. And when we are true to whom and to what we are and we are grateful for our being, we deploy our talents in ways that align with the universal Laws of Love and Good. It is then that God provides us the ways and the means to fulfill our goals.

We have vast resources of experience and wisdom in following Love's Light; when we go to the core of our power, our spiritual reserves, we muster those resources to refine our being and better meet life's challenges in the world head on.

So what is your gift, your talent? Are you using your gifts and talents in constructive ways? Are you fully expressing them? I am challenging all of you who are sitting on your big, fat talents because of some fear, to silence your reactive mind when it asks—*who am I to think that I can do this? Or, I don't have enough time. Or, I don't have the wherewithal to do what I know is mine to do.* Pray from the place of your passion and conviction; start in gratitude, and get in touch with that positive feeling. Reflect daily on that for which you are grateful.

In spite of the overwhelming obstacles, Sonia completed the filming of her movie. She used her gifts of acting, directing, writing and story-telling. Hers were not wasted. Do not waste yours.

Affirmation

Amen, Amen my life is a blessed life. And I am grateful for it all, especially my God-given talents and gifts. I use them to make a positive difference whenever and wherever I can.

Gratitude Raises Our Vibration

*Gratitude opens the door to the power, creativity and wisdom of
the entire Universe. We open the door through gratitude.*
DEEPAK CHOPRA

The Latin root of the word gratitude is *grata*—a given gift—and from
this same root we get the word *grace,* meaning a gift freely given that is
unearned. The *International Encyclopedia of Ethics* defines gratitude as "the
heart's internal indicator on which the tally of gifts outweighs exchanges."

Gratitude is also a feeling that spontaneously emerges from within.
However, it is not simply an emotional response; it is rather a choice we
make. We can choose to be grateful, or we can choose to be ingrates
by taking our gifts and blessings for granted. It is also an attitude or
disposition and a state of being that is essential to a life well lived.

The expression of gratitude continues to be the glue that consistently
holds society and relationships together. Gratitude's opposite—
ungratefulness – contributes to societal dysfunction, dissolution, and
perceptions of separation from our Creator. I believe the expression
of gratitude is essential to humankind's sustainability and survival.
Its stabilizing and healing effects have been researched from multiple
standpoints—cultural, psychological, spiritual, physiological and even
financial—and the results of that research make clear the benefits of living
a grateful life: gratitude raises our vibration.

Why Vibe-High? In his book *Power vs. Force* Dr. David Hawkins states
that there is a hierarchy of vibration, with matter (dense energy) at the
low end and energy (uncondensed matter) at the higher end. Divine Mind

is even higher than energy. The level where the conditions and earthly treasures may be gained is at the higher vibratory levels. The ancient teachings say, "All manifestation of thought, emotion, reason, will, or desire, or any mental state or condition are accompanied by vibrations." These vibrations are, in a sense, transmitted to the area around them in the same way heat radiates outward and upward from its source.

Every one of our thoughts, emotions, and mental states has a corresponding rate and mode of vibration. Vibrations are frequencies and can be changed by a change in the thought patterns which inhabit our minds. Since the Universe is also made up of vibrations at the deepest level, and the matter that is the Universe can be affected and changed just by our attention, the vibration of our thoughts has the power to affect the very substance of the Universe. That is why people situated in different places around the globe pray simultaneously for world peace. They believe that collective prayer changes vibration. The Universe is like the body in that respect. It will give us what we dwell upon, be it negativity or optimism. The thinker will attract what he thinks most about.

Every thought and every mood has its corresponding vibration. To change mood or mental state, one just has to change his vibration. For example, when I was grieving the loss of my husband, I used to play our wedding song over and over and over. I would become sad and tearful, longing for what I used to have. One day my nine-year-old daughter Briana, walked into my room, ejected the CD, and unceremoniously said, "Change your mood. Listen to music that makes you happy, not sad, Mommy." She then ran out of the room, giggling while chasing her soccer ball.

The closer two things harmonize or are complementary, the stronger the attraction between them. This principle is also known as *sympathetic resonance* or "like attracts like" and is the basis behind this interaction. The world we create or attract to us is the one that most closely aligns with our thought atmosphere. The chorus of our vibrational pattern of beliefs, emotions, and being determines the reality we experience. If we are feeding our fears, then that is the chord that is being sung and energized. That energized chord will find corresponding chords in the Universe and "sing" with them. Who and what we choose to "sing" with is determined by the chords we choose to play and invigorate.

The advantages of a hi-vibe life are many. Physical healing is an obvious one. Disease cannot exist in high vibration tissue. Mental and emotional healing is another advantage of living a hi-vibe life. Finding forgiveness, practicing gratitude, and healing addictions and old wounds are all characteristics of hi-vibe living. Spiritual growth is also enhanced, allowing us to experience a deeper connection with God, leading to a greater sense of peace and well-being.

Grateful thinking and grateful living promote the relishing of positive life experiences. By appreciating and taking pleasure in the blessings in our life we will be able to extract maximum fulfillment and enjoyment from our current circumstances. In the words of Lynn Twist, author of *The Soul of Money*, "What we appreciate appreciates."

Expressing gratitude bolsters our self-esteem and self-worth. When we realize how much we have accomplished, overcome, or withstood, we feel more confident knowing that we have the power to produce our desired results.

We create our own reality. As everything is connected and human thought creates on the etheric plane, we know that conditions can be manifested into the physical world by holding the right intention with the right attitude and thoughts. We can co-create with the Universe to realize our ideal life.

Having a higher vibration increases our manifesting power on all levels, and gratitude is an emotional vibration that makes it easier to attract what we want. By expressing gratitude for that which has not yet materialized, we are adopting a posture of assuming that what we want we already have. For instance, if we are grateful for our relationships and express this gratitude, the vibration of love is amplified and, in turn, serves to increase the flow of loving relationships into our life experience. It must then also be true that if we are grateful for good health, our body will respond and more good health will be the result.

What can we do to raise our vibratory level? The first step to raising our vibration is to remove from our life the things that might be keeping it low. Lifestyle choices and stress can have particularly strong effects on our vibration. Entrapped emotions will also hold our vibration down, particularly anxiety and depression.

Exposure to negativity such as toxins in our food and toxic people lower our vibration. Toxic people are those who consistently hold negative thoughts toward others and who are critical and void of compassion. They tend to vibrate at lower frequencies. It would serve us all well to disengage or limit our interactions with them.

Energy work, including Japanese energy healing modalities such as Jorei and Reiki, and meditation can help raise vibration. Reflexology, aromatherapy, and massage have tested strong for most people and can have very beneficial effects, as well. Being outdoors, communing with nature, and getting regular exercise raise vibration too.

And, of course, gratitude – gratitude has been shown to be the most potent way to raise one's vibration. Joy and happiness are what we feel when we are grateful, and these emotions naturally elevate our consciousness. Acknowledging that we have more for which to be grateful increases our faith in God and life improves, as Cause and Effect are forever at work.

Gratitude teaches us to appreciate all that is and all that we have. It allows us to fully appreciate life, existence, and that ultimate sense of belonging. Gratitude raises our vibratory level to a place whereby we can accept the whole of this given Universe. When we vibrate at the level of gratitude, we are fully one with the Whole—One with God.

Gratitude opens the doors to the power, creativity, and wisdom of the entire Universe to us. Just imagine that.

Affirmation

I am grateful for everything I experience in this lifetime. With gratitude as a way of life I vibrate at high levels, attracting corresponding experiences into my life.

Part V

GRACE, LOVE & FORGIVENESS

Tale of Two Sisters

For by grace you have been saved through faith; it is a gift of God.
EPHESIANS 2:8

For more than two months while facilitating a course on practical mysticism I focused on living the life of a modern day mystic. So what exactly does that mean? To me, it means to live in grace. It means that as one who connects regularly to her Higher Power and endeavors to live life from an elevated state of consciousness, she avails herself to God's Grace. I have become more and more aware of God's continual, unfailing, and unearned favor upon my life. As a consequence and because I recognize the privileged life I live, I have decided that I must pay grace forward. I am compelled to give to the world that which God continuously gives me. By doing so, I live a life of grace, using this energy to heal, express joy and bring things into more wholeness.

According to the founder of Religious Science, Ernest Holmes, grace is not something imposed upon us; it is the logical result of the correct acceptance of and the correct relationship to God. I would like to share with you a "Tale of Two Sisters" a story that illustrates how we are saved by Grace to the extent that we believe in, accept, and seek to embody it while using universal laws to our advantage, in this case, the Law of Good. Grace is the Law of Good actuated in our lives.

I recently visited the Orient—Narita, Shanghai and Hangzhou. I went at the invitation of my "sister friend" Renee, whom I have known for more than forty years. She accepted an overseas "gig" to perform nightly at a jazz club in Hangzhou, a small city an hour bullet train ride from Shanghai.

Just before my departure, I received a disturbing email from her. Renee was depressed because of the racism and blatant harassment she was subjected to, upon her arrival in Hangzhou. She said that she couldn't take much more of the fondling from men who, because they viewed her merely as an object, not a person, grabbed at her at will. Adults and children alike imitated monkeys and pointed to her and laughed. Someone actually spat on her in disgust. She forgot about God's grace which is the assistance God gives us when we elect to become the people that He means us to be even in the face subhuman treatment. God's grace enables us to endure unbelievable hardships.

I affirmed before my sojourn that her experience would not be my experience. It is because of the Grace of God that I can travel anywhere in the world I choose. God has bestowed unearned favor upon me, and I don't take my good fortune for granted.

So, upon arrival in Hangzhou I began my "Grace Experiment." When people stared at me I would smile and wave at them. Nine out of ten times they smiled and waved back. Foreigners, especially black ones, are a rarity in Hangzhou. Maybe I am naïve, but I believe that most people are just curious. To satisfy their curiosity and to dispel the myths about black people to which they have been brainwashed by the media, I decided to be the light that illuminates their dark perceptions of blacks and black women in particular.

I decided to pay grace forward—the Grace and favor that God has showered upon me. I had no idea of how to do this, but when I intuited something, I did it. For instance, I spent the day at West Lake, thought to be the most beautiful place in Hangzhou. It is the hub of community life for the residents of this city. Folks gather to dance, relax, stroll, sail, and picnic each day. On Monday they line danced Chinese style. I watched them from afar. On Tuesday, when they hand-danced, I couldn't contain myself and decided to join them. Spirit said "jump in and dance." I am an obedient servant, so I stood at the edge of the circle and began to move to the music. The next thing I know I was pulled to the center and all eyes were on me. I danced and smiled and invited others to dance with me. Folks on the edge clapped, laughed, smiled, and mimicked my movements. I wasn't successful in getting them to learn the Wobble, the latest line dance in the states, but they did free-style with me. This went on for about thirty minutes until I was drenched with perspiration after having danced with several partners, each having lined up to take their turn to dance with the "foreigner with the temperature hovering around 90 degrees and the humidity even higher." I became a celebrity of sorts. When folks saw me on the streets the days after we danced, they smiled, pointed and waved. Not once was anyone mean or rude to me.

I tell you this story because it is the tale of two sisters in one city who had two completely different realities. I thoroughly enjoyed my time in Hangzhou while my sister friend couldn't wait to leave that "hub of barbarians with their lack of social graces and ignorance."

Later, on the day of my dance debut, a gorgeous African-American woman in her mid-twenties approached me while I was dining at a Sushi bar. She walked over and introduced herself as Melissa and said that she was curious about me. She assumed that I was American and wondered why I was in Hangzhou. We chatted, and that evening she joined me to hear Renee perform at JZ, the gathering place for foreigners and expats where they can hear American music, jazz in particular, and eat French fries and burgers.

Because I wanted Renee to know someone else in the city who was having a positive experience, I introduced her to Melissa, who had lived there for more than six months. Melissa invited us to church. She attended a diverse church where foreign passport-holders gather each Sunday to worship in "the Word" as she referred to the service. Natives were not allowed. When she extended an invitation to Renee, Renee agreed to go but with this disclaimer: "I am a cussing, smoking, drinking, sinning soul who doesn't practice any religion." Melissa said: "No matter; you are still most welcome." As it turned out, I went alone, and of course had a wonderful time.

I choose to live a life of Grace by seeing the Good in everything. My glass of life is half full. Renee's glass, maybe...not so much.

Weekly affirmations are sent to ministers and practitioners from the home office of the spiritual organization of which I am affiliated. I chose this affirmation for my travels abroad to Asia: *I serve and am served by the gifts I have to give—the gifts given to me by the life I am privileged to live.*

I served the people of Hangzhou by sharing my gift of light, love of life, and dance. I know among those with whom I danced, that they will have a different perception of black women in the future. They now know that there can be unity even within our diversity. They now know that we do have some things in common and that we are human beings just as they are, that is, living life in our own unique ways. Not to mention that they now have a few new, soulful dance moves! I know that I have left a legacy of love that transcends language, race, culture, nationality, politics, and gender.

I implore you to live Grace. Be Grace wherever you are and whenever there is an opportunity. Living in grace means that you exhibit your unique personality by sharing yourself--giving yourself over to whatever goodness you are able to create or sustain. This kind of grace comes with the awareness that you are participating in the very Life of God. See the Good in all things.

Affirmation

My faith comes from the certainty of God's Grace. I practice, embody and extend grace wherever I am. I am a steward of God's Grace in the world.

Loved from Afar

To forgive is to set a prisoner free and discover that the prisoner was you.
LOUIS B. SMEDES

It was a blustery fall day when my father tried to take his life. I had already lost him to the depression that faded his smile and dulled his spirit for eight years. I grieved the loss of his vitality and bubbly personality. I had to accept the fact that the father that he had been was no more. Fortunately, I visited him that day and found him unconscious with an empty bottle of sleeping pills on his night stand. Thank God that the expiration date had passed and the pills had lost their potency! I was able to wake him and called 911. He was rushed to Montgomery County General Hospital in Olney, Maryland, where he was hospitalized or treated as an outpatient for nearly four months.

While there, my father endured individual and group therapy. He never shared with others and complained that their "depressing" stories were more than he could bear. He just sat quietly and listened. He was a private, withdrawn man in his old age, to a point of becoming a recluse. He first withdrew from his friends and neighbors, then his church community, the world and finally from the rest of the family. I was tolerated because I was his caregiver and the manager of his finances.

When life nipped at my heels, I would go to him and lay my burdens at his feet. With soft brown eyes full of love, compassion and concern he would sit in silence and listen without judgment. His sweet silence was balm to my soul. Sometimes he would offer words laced with regret that he couldn't do more.

As the years passed, Dad became less able to care for himself. As his health declined his dependency on me increased, so did his stubbornness. It was that obstinacy that lit up his soul. His stubbornness kept the embers of life burning within him, and I could see the happy, gregarious, loquacious, fast walking father that I once knew and loved.

As he aged decades in less than five years, his taste buds dulled. He craved extremely spicy or syrupy sweet food. I remember him asking me to bring him a butter pound cake the next time I shopped. A day or so later, I stopped by to drop off his sweet treat. I put the cake on the table and took leave to restore my personal comfort. When I returned only minutes later, he had devoured half of it with his hands. Many of the crumbs stuck to his beard. Looking up at me with mischievous eyes, he was a sight to behold! I held up a mirror for him to see just how ridiculous he looked. We both laughed long and hardy that day.

I remember a more recent time when my children and I visited him in the nursing home which became his permanent residence after a bad fall and spell of pneumonia. He was on a bland diet, and the meat was pureed and sculpted to resemble what it was supposed to be--a lamb chop or maybe a veal cutlet. At one point, he leaned over and whispered to my son Sharif, "I want some Popeyes," the Louisiana style fried chicken. Did I mention that Dad lived at the Hebrew Home of Greater Washington where non-kosher foods were not allowed? Dad looked so pitiful that day that my daughter Briana and I went on a covert mission to score some Popeyes. We snuck the chicken into his room and served up tiny pieces of breast and spoons full of red beans and rice—his heaven-scent manna. It was a pleasure to see the sparkle return to his lifeless eyes. Our covert operations ended abruptly when the attending nurse smelled the aroma of that spicy fried chicken. She admonished us for feeding him food not on his diet and for bringing non-kosher food on property! That escapade gave my father a few laughs and us a fond memory when I visited with him over the next few weeks. That joyful day was the last time the four of us were together.

I smile as I write this story because the memories of my father keep him alive to me. I can look all around my home and see things that he either gave me or made for me during the twenty-five years that he lived with or near me. Our relationship ended well though it wasn't always this way.

In March 1963, my father vanished without a trace. I was a young girl when he no longer showed up for occasional Sunday dinners at Big Mama's house in Los Angeles. I recount writing in my diary about my "deadbeat dad." I resented him for disappearing but mostly for not being around to stand up for me against my stepfather, who in my opinion was definitely qualified to be a prison warden. Al was mean and avoided all of my protests to spare the rod. With my pen, I called my father a coward, a no good bum and included him in the statistics of absentee fathers that I often overheard single-mothers complaining about!

As mysteriously as my father had vanished, magically he reappeared unapologetic and unannounced many years later. By that time I had my own house, hearth and husband. After work one day, there was an old motor home parked on our property. I recall yelling to my husband as I entered the front door, "Whose contraption is that parked in our driveway?" When I got to the kitchen Thomas was in deep conversation with a man I didn't know but who vaguely resembled my estranged father. I wasn't sure because my memory of him had dimmed over time. But sure enough, Thomas introduced this man to me, my father, James, and informed me that he would be staying with us permanently. My face reddened, my hands became sweaty, and my heart raced as I absorbed this bizarre moment. Then my temper erupted like an active volcano, as I spewed remarks about "allowing a perfect stranger into our home!" I lost that battle.

Over the next few weeks, James spent his days cooking up favorites from our roots in New Orleans like gumbo, jambalaya and pralines with pecans. He won our affection through our stomachs. He also acquired a new name in the process—Grandpa. Though he was my father, I referred to him as Grandpa like the children did.

Hyped with excitement in the sweltering summer of August 1993, the kids, Grandpa and I moved to 'New Havana'--my name for Miami's southwest quadrant. Thomas commuted between California and Florida due to work demands. My husband morphed into 'the estranged father' as Grandpa transformed into the surrogate father to my children. In 1994, Thomas took his own life leaving me to raise our children alone. After his untimely death, my heart was heavy with grief and all the responsibility that comes with being a single parent in a foreign land. In my father's efforts to assuage my fears, he promised to be there for me and my children for as long as he lived--a promise that he kept. Life for us came full circle with Dad caring for my children then me caring for him during the sunset of his eighty-six-year existence.

Life is a great teacher. I learned the art of forgiveness by cultivating a relationship with my father. I freed myself from my self-constructed prison. I was liberated from the bondage of my childhood resentments simply because I let them go. Together, Dad and I wrote new stories about unconditional love and commitment. He became father to my children and best friend to me but that didn't happen without work. It happened because I set that intention. I then allowed my relationship with my father to merely unfold. His daily presence and dedication to the love and care of my family erased my memory of ever being abandoned. I forgot, and forgave him and myself for the past while focusing my energy on reconciliation. Sometimes the temptation to dwell on the past was present which I worked hard to resist. And it is through the transformation of our relationship that my heart softened and my former feelings of desertion dissolved to nothingness.

When a loved one dies, it is natural for the human heart to grieve the loss of their physical presence. In truth, it is not the physical presence which wins our love. Dad's loving heart and caring soul drew forth my love. I miss my father's unselfish devotion to me and my children. And it is in my remembering that he will always be with me forever loving me from afar.

Affirmation:

As I follow the path of forgiveness, I set my past free and forgive myself for holding resentments. As my heart opens, I am free to give and receive love. Love truly does conquer all.

Living Grace

It's not the law of religion, nor the principles of morality that define
our highways and pathways to God; only by the Grace of God
are we led and drawn to God.
It is His grace that conquers a multitude of flaws
and in that grace there is only favor.
Favor is not achieved; favor is received.

C. JOYBELL C

Grace has been defined as the impersonal outpouring of God's Love into Its creation—an unearned favor and a gift of God. It is God's continual, unfailing faithfulness to His creation. Grace teaches us how to live and how to extend grace to others.

Living grace, like any new behavior, takes practice. The adage "practice makes permanent" embodies one of the great laws of human nature, and as a law it is never under any circumstances broken. There is no achievement without practice.

Living grace begins when you grace others with your presence. Take time to be with people in times of need. Just being present demonstrates that you love them, and most often that is more than enough. Living grace is bearing witness to others' accomplishments and acting genuinely as happy for them as you would be if you had achieved an important goal of your own.

Forgive with grace. When someone offers you an apology, accept it graciously. They have come to you humbly asking for your pardon. It is, therefore, neither a time to reprove them nor a time to set them right by telling them how they could have handled a situation differently. Allow them to see that you have accepted their apology.

Take the time to say "thank you." It doesn't cost anything, but expressing thanks can show other people your gratitude and grace. Write a simple card expressing your appreciation for a kind act on your behalf. You can make a world of difference by simply putting a "thank you" on your lips or on paper.

Have you ever been criticized by someone? If you don't like the way in which the feedback was given, you can respond in a gracious way. Accept what they have to say and thank them for their input. The news they bring you may indeed upset you and even hurt you deeply. The way you respond, however, can help the healing process within you to begin immediately. Respond with grace.

On the other hand, a quick angry response will leave you seething. So the sooner you can respond with a smile and a calm spirit, the sooner you will be able to discern any truth in their words and make changes that you can agree need to be made.

When you need to apologize, don't delay. What's more, don't keep a running tab of how many times someone has wronged you. Forgive them, even if they don't ask to be forgiven. Grace can go a long way in repairing a relationship if you respond in a loving way, even when the other party doesn't. Keep short accounts.

When speaking to others, use words that are kind and gentle. Obviously there are times we need to correct other people, but it never has to be done in a hateful or mean-spirited way. Find a way to gently say what needs to be said. Use "I" statements to describe how you feel, taking full responsibility for your feelings. With this approach you are less likely to put the other person on the defensive. Show grace with your words.

Can you help someone in some small way? Holding a door for someone whose arms are full can be a small action that helps in a great way. By seeking out little actions you can do for others, you are well on your way to becoming a more graceful person. Don't just look for opportunities to fulfill monumental needs. One's ability to change other people's lives with large financial donations or heroic actions is seldom within the average person's grasp; but simple kindnesses can go a long way to affect the lives of others in a positive way. Be aware of the needs of others.

Certainly it is appropriate to respond to questions when people ask you about yourself, but try to ask a few questions of your own in return to learn about other people. In the words of Stephen R. Covey, seek first to understand then to be understood. When you let people talk about themselves, be sincerely interested in their responses. Show interest in others.

Happiness is the spiritual experience of living every minute with love and grace. Yrjo Kallinen described grace in one of his writings as something that transcends and overcomes everything. Grace is a gift from God that unites us with Life and with our higher selves. Grace has transformative powers and the word itself possesses something victorious within it.

Practice being the presence of grace wherever you are: speak words of grace, say "thank you," take interest in others, seek first to understand, forgive gracefully, keep short accounts of offenses, and be quick to forgive others as well as yourself.

Ask yourself: *To whom can I express grace today? Or, Who can I forgive today?*

Affirmation

When I forgive, grace is present. When I listen, grace is present. When I aid another, grace is present. The Grace of God is upon me always and I lovingly extend it to others.

Love and Passion

We love life, not because we are used to *living but because we are used to loving.*
FRIEDRICH NIETZSCHE

What does it mean to "live from love?" Have you placed your "true loves" on the altar of your life? Are you living from your loves and passions?

Living from love entails loving yourself first and then extending that love to others. Living from love also means practicing: acceptance, forgiveness, non-judgment, and compassion with one another. Living from love of oneself is positive self-regard in action. It's about loving yourself enough to act on the things for which you are passionate.

Finding and living your life passion is one of the most important endeavors you will ever undertake and one of the highest forms of self-love. There is a process to uncovering your "true love" and living your passion. It isn't hard, but it does take commitment, patience, and determination. After spending some time engaged in "visioning" (a process whereby we listen for Divine Guidance), *compose a vision statement.* Write down exactly what you want your life to look like in every area. Examine your current life to see how much of it matches your vision. Maintain those valuable assets and have faith that aspects of your vision are already happening. *Define your values.* Make sure you are clear on the core values you will live by. Every decision you make about your passion and how you want your life to look should support or reflect those values. Then, *take action.* Taking the first real action toward your dream might seem daunting. It might mean taking a course, securing financing for your business concept, volunteering to gain experience, or moving beyond the

"Land of the Familiar" by stepping outside of your comfort zone. Your first action says to you, "I'm committed to living the life of my dreams."

Once you are living your passion, the quality of your life will improve dramatically. When you are doing something you love, that is, something you feel deeply about, everything feels more joyful. And it is from that joy that you have the wherewithal to extend love to others. Erich Fromm, psychologist and social philosopher, proposed that loving oneself entails caring about oneself, taking responsibility for oneself, respecting oneself, and knowing oneself. He further proposed that to be able to truly love another person, a person needs first to love himself in this way. The lyrics to a simple song we sing to our first-time guests each Sunday sums it up: "I love myself so much that I can love you so much."

Love is often described in terms of feelings. But true love—what the Greeks termed *agape love*—is not based on feelings at all. Agape is love which is of and from God, whose very nature is love itself. Agape love can change your life and set you free. It all begins with your decision to consider the needs of others; that is, to give without demanding a return or to overlook offenses and thereby forgive others. *Forgiveness* is the intentional and voluntary process by which the offended undergoes a change in feelings and attitude regarding an offense and then lets go of negative emotions such as anger, and embraces the ability to bless the offender. Anger and blame are unproductive emotions that tie up energy in destroying rather than creating new life. Living from love requires loving those who have harmed you too, and expressing your empathy toward them. Studies show that people who forgive others are happier and healthier than those who hold onto resentments.

In his book, *The Awakened Heart: Opening Yourself to the Love You Need*, Gerald C. May states that, "All of us desire love and our true identity, and our reason for being is to be found in this desire." He goes on to say that, "Love is the "why" of life and it is the fundamental energy of what the human spirit is. Love is what makes all goodness even possible."

Thus, living from love is a perspective, a way of being and is essential for individual flourishing. It demands that your "true loves" be placed at the very center of your life. When you vibrate at the level of love, love quite simply radiates from you, and through grace that love is expressed to others and manifested in the things of which you are passionate. That's the way the Universe works.

Affirmation

I freely bestow the gift of love to others without exception or expectation. I express love through the work that ignites from passion within me. Love always returns good to me, pressed down and running over.

Part VI

SELF-INQUIRY: DISCOVERING YOUR HIGHER SELF

Deep Inquiry: Surfacing the Life Within

...the greatest good of man is daily to converse about virtue, and
all that concerning which you hear me examining myself and others,
and that the life which is unexamined is not worth living.
SOCRATES

During my ministerial training I was introduced to a process of deep inquiry in a spiritual counseling class. The class was designed so that the student assumed the roles of both minister and client. We asked deep questions to uncover the parts of ourselves which we either chose to deny or endeavored to forget because the choices we made were not from our Higher Self. We documented both the questions and the answers in a journal and were encouraged to write and write and write until eventually there was nothing left to write about. At the moment when we thought there was nothing left to say, we were challenged to ask ourselves, "Is there anything else?" And when a question is put into the universe, the mind searches for an answer, and just when we thought we had exhausted every possible thought about the question, more ideas came to us.

Deep inquiry is a path to self-discovery, attained through meditation and spiritual discernment. This practice of making an inward turn has been used for centuries by different cultures, religions, and spiritual traditions. In Advaita-Vedanta teaching, for example, the goal of deep inquiry or self-examination is the whole experience of the non-dual self—not separated from the Creator or one another. Inquiry into the nature of the self is the chosen path. The ultimate goal might best be described as the resolution of the mind in its Source that is God, the Self.

I have found tremendous value in this process, and once on this path there was no turning back. Why is that? Once devoted to this practice, it became a meditative process that altered my state of mind, freeing me from my experiences of conditions and circumstances. Advaita-Vedanta teaching explains this phenomenon in this way: when the mind identifies the self with the "not-self" (the body, life conditions, etc.), there is bondage. When this wrong identification is removed through repetitive self-inquiry ("Who am I? Why do I exist?"), there is release—freedom from limiting thoughts and beliefs.

Deep self-inquiry differs significantly from what typically happens in our minds. Our minds inquire into the effects, facts, circumstances, and conditions we experience. For instance, when something that we don't want to happen in our lives actually does happen, the first question that most ask is, "Why is this happening to me?" The mind seeks an answer that, upon examination, will be found to be merely its own projection; it does not reflect on itself or trace itself to its source. The true answer can be found through deep inquiry by turning the mind away from the condition and inward to our Higher Self. Self-inquiry is not the mind's inspection of itself. When correctly practiced, tenacious deep inquiry ceases to exist and the Higher Self emerges. Deep inquiry gives constant attention to, and an awareness of, the "I AM."

Affirmation:

Through self-inquiry my search is over. I have discovered the great "I AM," and today I speak and live this Reality in every experience I have. The "I AM" is reflected in me in every way.

Internal Review: A Path to Success

Look well into thyself; there is a source of strength which
will always spring up if thou wilt always look there.
MARCUS AURELIUS

I invite you to pause and take a close look at the events in your life for their implications. In their book, *The Joyous Living Journal,* Reverends Weldes and Sorensen (two colleagues of mine) ask a profound question about internal review: "What within you has attracted the failures and disappointments into your life—the positive or the soul-searching thoughts?" Or the self-talk that tells you that you are not enough? "If it's one of those soul-stretching times that challenge the very fabric of your faith, start looking at the behaviors or attitudes that might have contributed to the energy-depleting experience in which you find yourself."

Those soul-searching times of challenge are not the times to be dishonest with oneself. They are the times to conduct a brutally honest internal review. Feelings might surface from deep within—fears, doubts, lack of self-confidence, shame, or even guilt. What is valuable about this discovery is that through the inquiry process you can determine whether any of those emotions played a role in what you are experiencing now and whether they are points of concern deep in your subjective mind. Wouldn't it be of benefit to clear up those debilitating thoughts, feelings and emotions?

In the parable of the talents which I am contemporizing for expediency, Jesus tells the story of a certain nobleman who went abroad to obtain power for himself. Before he left, he called ten of his servants, giving them each a one hundred dollar bill and telling them, "Trade with this until I come back." When he returned, he ordered his servants to be brought before him for their report.

You know the story: the first servant increased the original one hundred dollars, as did the second. The third servant responded with a speech which really was an excuse. (Rationalization is something many of us use for not doing what we intended to do.) "I kept it safe, folded it in a napkin, and hid it under my mattress." The nobleman was incensed. He ordered the servant to leave at once!

The unfortunate servant was not cast off because he failed to realize any profit for the nobleman. No. He was cast off because he did not "work" at it. Truly knowing ourselves requires effort. Realizing our dreams requires work. We must be vigilant in our resolve to grow into self-fulfillment. We are never under any external obligation to achieve results for which we set our personal goals and intentions. Results are not mandatory for anyone but ourselves if we are sincere in our desires to be successful, however we define success for ourselves. No one likes to fail, but the surest way to fail is to not do the work necessary to become successful. If the results we desire are left free to form themselves, in terms of the quality of life we wish to attain, then the likelihood of achieving or manifesting that life remains elusive to us.

The shadow self inhibits us and is mainly composed of all of our suppressed and negative emotions and feelings. It holds our outdated ideas and insecurities, feeding on discouragement, fears, and doubts. The shadow self grows each time we dwell on our failures and lack confidence in our own abilities. It is the opposite of who we truly are and works against what we consciously desire. It gains power when we deny its existence and will attempt to dominate and control our lives. The shadow self wants us to fail. In order to move beyond it in the pursuit and attainment of our goals, dreams and desires, we must learn to recognize the shadow and confront it. To disempower the shadow self at the point of confrontation is the most we can do. It will always lurk in the darkest recesses of our subconscious as we move beyond the perimeter of what we already know into the unchartered waters of our future.

I've learned from the sages of the past that the true path to enlightenment requires the total acceptance of the shadow self. This process of total acceptance or soul integration includes all aspects of our being—both positive and negative. In order to become whole, healthy, complete beings, we need to face our shadow selves and compassionately accept and heal the lost fragments of consciousness. This requires digging deep within, observing and confronting our wounded human self, offering it solace and compassion, and then releasing it. Facing up to the shadow self is vital for self-fulfillment, though it can be a process that is distressing and most uncomfortable.

The good news is that the human soul possesses an astonishing and very real capacity for self-reflection, analysis, and forgiveness. Every layer of shadow that we probe, uncover, heal, and integrate will raise our energetic vibration. As we let go of more and denser, obstructed shadow energy, we begin to feel lighter physically and emotionally. We have loftier thoughts and healthier emotions that cause positive sensations in our bodies and manifestations in our affairs. As we convert our low-vibrational shadow into Light, we enhance our physical health and well-being. Each time we merge more of our hidden consciousness into the Light, we are piecing back together our whole self and reconnecting to the Divine Presence and the Wholeness in our human experience. Darkness has been defined as the absence of Love. If this holds true, then the most effective tonic to use in healing our internal shadow is self-love. The more love we flow into our deepest wounds and darkest emotions, the quicker we are able to clear and raise our vibration.

In his book, *This Thing Called You*, Ernest Holmes, an international authority on religious psychology, wrote "Know that your words of prayer dissolve every negative thought or impulse that could throw a shadow over your perfection."

Take the time to ask yourself the hard questions about the stories you make up that don't add to but rather subtract from the quality of your life. Reviewing the decisions you made in the past and then releasing all guilt associated with the bad ones will free you up to move forward. Look deep into yourself and tap into the source of strength you will always find exists there. Internal review is a tool for self-transformation.

Affirmation

Today I uncover the perfection within me. I look upon the world of my affairs knowing that the Spirit within makes my way immediate and easy. I know there is nothing in me that could possibly obstruct or withhold the Divine Circuit of Life, success, and prosperity from me. Light casts out all shadows.

Mental Freedom

Forces beyond your control can take away everything you possess
except one thing—your freedom to choose your attitude
in any given set of circumstances, to choose one's way.
VIKTOR E. FRANKL

As a long-time prisoner in four concentration camps, Viktor Frankl was stripped to naked existence. He was, however, mentally free, which means that he had a clearer expression of the constructive qualities of his mind. He controlled his own thoughts though he had no other basic freedoms. He said, "There is nothing in the world, I venture to say, that would so effectively help one to survive even the worst conditions, as the knowledge that there is a meaning to one's life. Meaning can be discovered by the attitude we take toward unavoidable suffering."

In theology it is said that God gave us choice and free will. Free will is the apparent human ability to make choices. And Jewish philosophy stresses that free will is a faculty intrinsic to humans and that the ability to make a free choice is through the part of the soul that is united with God, the only being that is not hindered by, or dependent on, cause and effect.

Nelson Mandela's story of being incarcerated at Robben Island, a prison in South Africa, further illustrates these ideas of mental freedom, choice, and free will.

He lived for 18 of his 27 prison years in a small cell with only a twin-sized bed and a bucket for his bodily wastes. I stood in that cell while visiting South Africa with my family in 2007. It was depressing and claustrophobic. I couldn't imagine living in such poor conditions for more than a few minutes let alone nearly two decades. Mandela became the master of his own prison while there by focusing his energy on writing and strategically planning how to bring about a democratic South Africa. He emerged as a mature political leader who forgave his oppressors and fought many political battles that eventually eradicated apartheid.

Long before Mandela's birth, Plato said that "One cannot make a slave of a free person, for a free person is free even in a prison." In other words, we either choose freedom or create our own personal prisons. We unknowingly impose limitations upon ourselves through our restrictive, restraining thoughts and beliefs.

If you are unsure of what you truly believe, look at your life. Want a different life? Deliberately change your thoughts and beliefs. Beliefs do change as we grow in knowledge and experience. This is true for every one of us. At one time it was believed that the world was flat. With more knowledge and information, that belief, a belief held collectively in the consciousness of the human race, finally changed. With more knowledge of the Divine and more experience or demonstrations of spiritual truths playing out in our lives, we too can, and most likely will, change our beliefs about what is possible.

Our innate freedom is to choose how to respond to the occurrences in our lives, as was the case in Mandela's and Frankl's stories. We also know that we can influence conditions and circumstances through our thoughts, before we even experience them. When we align with the Divine, the only force that is not influenced by cause and effect, we can transcend the world.

Mental freedom is also about becoming free from the narrow confines of fear, doubt, worry, and lack. In contrast, mental slavery is being in a state of subjection and implies that one's thoughts are being controlled by something outside of us or that someone else is in control.

Instead, we can choose to live from our conscious awareness of our Authentic Self—our true nature of wholeness—offspring of the Divine. No one can liberate us mentally except ourselves.

Gandhi said, "The moment the slave resolves that he will no longer be a slave, his fetters fall. Freedom and slavery are mental states." Do you choose to live your life in your, self constructed cell of smallness? Or do you choose you to live your dreams? Either way, the choice is yours to make.

Affirmation

Today I choose mental freedom. I have the freedom to choose and to enjoy living. I am free to love and be loved. I am free to give full expression to every capacity I possess.

Part VII

THE POWER OF INTENTION

From Intention to Manifestation

Intention is one of the most powerful forces there is.
What you mean when you do a thing will always determine the outcome.
The law creates the world.
BRENNA YOVANOFF

A working definition of *intention* is to have in mind a purpose or plan by which to direct the mind and behaviors toward fulfillment of that plan. The dictionary definition of *intention* is that it is an act or instance of determining mentally some action or result; a determination to act in a certain way. Intention is the high resolve that the African American theologian Howard Thurman wrote about.

According to Wayne Dyer, author of *The Power of Intention*, intentions come from a deep place inside and are focused more on the present than on the end result. Once you have made a declaration of intention. On the other hand, Ernest Holmes, also emphasized in his book, *The Original Science of Mind*, how "the Thing Itself works with us and through us" and that the seed of perfection is hidden within us, meaning that all we need to succeed is within us. He goes on to say that, "the sum total of all of our thought, will, purpose, and belief creates a tendency in the Law that causes it to react to us according to the sum total of that belief." Holmes didn't actually use the term intention. However, his words are closely aligned with its definition as an act of mental determination.

Dyer states that ". . . the power of intention is one of those things that are easy to underestimate." However, when we are intentional about something, all of our energy and efforts go toward its attainment. Therein lies its power." Ernest Holmes says something to the same effect: "We are surrounded by an Infinite Possibility. And as it passes into our being, It automatically becomes the law of our lives." In other words, what we believe begins to rule our life as the decisions we make and the paths we take.

We should be very mindful of what affect our beliefs are having on us. The one who wishes to demonstrate some particular good must become conscious of this exacting thing if he wishes to have it or experience it. Therefore, he must make his mind receptive to it, and he must do it carefully, wisely, deliberately and with total awareness. Our thought or intention should mark our every effort and positively accompany all of our statements that we impress upon the Law. There is power in our spoken word to create our realities.

Setting your intention is easy. All you need to do is to come up with a positive intention statement that sums up what you propose to do. Your positive intention statement should be personal and meaningful to you, and you must take your intention seriously. Speak it aloud. Feel the words as you speak it. Mean what you say. If your declaration of intention is sincere, it will be all the more powerful. It will instruct the Law of Manifestation to bring about that which you have spoken.

You might be wondering: What's the relationship between intention and manifestation? Carlos Castaneda, author of *The Active Side of Infinity*, explains it this way:

> "In the universe there is an immeasurable,
> indescribable force which shamans call intent,
> and absolutely everything that exists in the entire cosmos
> is attached to intent by a connecting link."

In other words, once you lock your intention in your mind, you ignite the Divine Creative Process; all thought is creative. Your thought then creates a mold in the Subjective, also referred to as the Law, into which your intent is accepted and poured. It sets in motion the Laws of Attraction, Cause and Effect, Correspondence and Manifestation, of course, according to your thought and word. The Law is the doer, and its business is to reflect in the world of effects the thoughts and intent you cast into it. Your thoughts and words have energy and power to co-create your life with the Universe. When you've made a clear, committed decision or set your intention, it will open the universal floodgates, bringing you all the resources you need, sometimes in seemingly mysterious or even impossible ways. That is the power of intention!

Five Steps from Intention to Manifestation:

1. Get clear about something you desire. Once an idea comes to you, meditate on it. Visualize it and set your intention to achieve it. Write it down! The act of writing it down provides you the opportunity to clarify it in order that you don't send mixed messages to the Universe.

2. Unleash your personal power. Your mind, belief, and personal will are key ingredients in helping you focus on your intent. If you can believe it, you can achieve it. You do not have to know how it is going to happen; all you have to know is that it will.

3. Keep it alive. This is when you keep your intent at the forefront of what you are doing. Remember to take action every day to make sure you're demonstrating your commitment to your intention. Acknowledge that you did what you said you would do and then take the next step. Whenever negative thoughts start to creep in, reaffirm your intention.

4. Remain centered in a state of restful awareness. Intention is much more powerful when it comes from a place of trust and acceptance than if it arises from a sense of skepticism and resistance. You must stay centered and refuse to be influenced by other people's uncertainties, criticisms, or doubts. Your Higher Self knows that all is well and will be well, even without you knowing the timing or the details of what will happen.

5. Detach from the outcome. Surrender your attachment to a specific result. Do you know that attachment is fear-based? Do you also know detachment is based on the unquestioning belief in the power of the Invisible Creative Force that supports all life? Intend for everything to work out as it should; then let go, let God, and allow opportunities and resources to come your way in support of your expressed intention.

Intention is one of the most powerful forces in the Universe. You and Universal Law create your world. The infallible way to ensure your greatest fulfillment is to live intentionally.

Affirmation

I set my intention toward that which aligns with my soul's purpose. I give thanks for the manifestation of my goals, dreams and aspirations which express my divinity.

A New Design for Life

Nothing lies beyond the scope of your ability.
The new design for living you create has no limitations.
Literally all the good things that life and the world offer
are yours to have and enjoy. But you need to recognize
them, accept them, and incorporate them into
the new design you are now going to create.
ERNEST HOLMES

It has been said: "Where you place your attention, you are placing your intention." I remind you of this truism; when the year ends the New Year—pregnant with possibility—begins. If you don't want to repeat the experiences of past years, then set your intention and place your attention on the experiences you desire. Setting your intention is crucial to creating positive experiences. Where we focus our attention builds an energy field that, by the Law of Attraction, draws to us that which we think about. Where we place our attention creates a pattern of possibility, and opportunity; and, like a knife, the Law of nature cuts both ways.

In his book *A New Design for Living*, Ernest Holmes says it this way: "Basically, all that we have to do is to learn to get rid of our fears and doubts, to remove all confusion and bewilderment, until at last we arrive where we want to be—no longer conditioned or controlled by any external situation whatsoever. This is where we start. This is the point of departure from being influenced by conditions to influencing conditions." Instead of being in the back seat of a directionless, driverless car with unforeseen hazards ahead, we find ourselves in the driver's seat, calm, cool, collected and intentional; and with a knowledge that Infinite Intelligence knows of where we want to go and how we are going to get there, we proceed carefully to guide and direct our way along the highways and byways of life.

We are so fortunate in that, by simply exercising our power of free will, we get to decide the way in which we live life. I invite you to take your mind off your problems and put them on God, the Good, and Omnipotent. Shift your attention from what's missing or what seems to be wrong to all that is right, and to appreciate that which you already have. It is within the force field of gratitude and appreciation that more and more good can be made manifest. When we vibrate at the high frequency of gratitude and appreciation we can create consciously and intentionally through our thoughts, words and deeds. Thoughts that are accompanied by large amounts of positive, grateful energy have a greater affect on our lives and the world.

Affirmation

I know that the Laws of God are good and perfect and these Laws are my consciousness, therefore manifesting as my experience now. I know that the nature of my thought externalizes itself to bring about conditions that correspond exactly to where I place my attention. I am so grateful for the happiness, the joy, the health, the wealth, and the people that have been attracted to me. I am in complete acceptance of that which I have designed as my life now. I let it be so.

Part VIII

EXPECTATION & FAITH

Positive Expectancy

An attitude of positive expectation is the mark of the superior personality.
BRANDON TRACY

In selecting the title for this piece, I was deliberate in adding the word "positive" before the word "expectancy" because many of us are expectant, but we expect the worst and therefore experience that which we don't want. Positive expectancy ignites the Law of Attraction. Like attracts like, and when we are expecting the best outcome we attract positive influences and positive situations, and in turn are drawn to positive results.

More than any other trait of human personality, an attitude of positive expectancy is the precursor to success in every achievement, every worthwhile venture, and every upward step in personal progress. Positive expectancy gives us the power of focus, and when we focus all our thoughts, plans, and actions on our goals, we are able to: 1) define our priorities, 2) overcome hurdles and obstacles, 3) maintain our enthusiasm, and 4) take responsibility for taking the actions necessary to achieve our goals. Because positive expectancy transforms us into movers, it also inspires us to use our imagination and creativity in constructive ways and impels us to take purposeful action. It increases our determination. It pushes us to further develop our potential. The Law of Expectancy works this way because mental images act as stimuli to both the conscious and subconscious mind and, therefore, corresponding actions follow.

To leverage the power of positive expectancy, begin to adopt the following:

1. a belief in yourself and your potential;
2. a belief in your faith;
3. a belief in infinite possibilities; and
4. a belief in the God Force and Its support of all of us in the attainment of our desires.

In *The Original Science of Mind*, Ernest Holmes states: "There is a Law of Attraction and Repulsion that works automatically. It is like the Law of Reflection where the reflection corresponds with the image held in front of the mirror." Jesus proclaimed that it is done unto us as we believe. This spiritual master and great example, even went so far as to say that when we feel the need of anything or desire it, we should pray for it, and in the act of our prayer we should mentally expect the object of our desire as though it already exists. This is the fundamental nature of the Laws of Attraction and Expectancy that act automatically upon our expectations.

How careful we must be to guard our thoughts and only expect good! This principle is true and its reward is certain. Nothing is more important than that we should consciously use the Law of Attraction, ignited by positive expectancy, to attain our hearts' desires. Positive expectancy comes from building a strong faith in God and is the character of a superior personality.

Affirmation:

I have faith in God and my own affirmations. I know there is a Power flowing through me, taking the form of my thoughts, beliefs and expectations. I affirm that every good thing I do will prosper.

The Joy of Expectation

Excellence is the result of caring more than others think is wise, risking more than others think is safe, dreaming more than others think is practical, and expecting more than others think is possible.
RONNIE OLDHAM

Expectancy means to have a strong desire and to be filled with anticipation and confidence that you will obtain what is desired. Like everything else in life, there is an energetic vibration associated with positive expectancy. That vibration is joy.

The joy of expectation is an emotion evoked by the prospect of possessing what one desires. Joy is both the source and the result of expectation. Joy and expectation are merged together at several pivotal points in the expectation journey. There is the joy that is evident when we first begin to have deep, positive expectations for the future. The joy of beginning is a true joy, but does not guarantee that the expectation will be fulfilled or that the joy felt at the beginning will be sustained. The joy of the successful journey is the joy that is evident as expectations are realized.

As a mother, I understand what it is like to experience joy because I have ushered new life into existence. I felt joy while expecting the birth of both of my children. In the case of expectant mothers, through the morning sickness, the swollen feet, and the back pain, we still wait with joyous expectation for our little "bundles of joy" to make their appearance on earth. And what I remember is the exhilaration and excitement that derived from my expectancy.

The Bible has many scriptures that encourage us to wait in joyous expectation of our hearts desires such as these:

2 Corinthians 9:8

And God is able to make all grace abound to you, so that having all sufficiency in all things at all times, you may abound in every good work.

This is another way of saying that once you set your intention and expect fulfillment of that intention the Universe will support you—having all sufficiency in all things at all times.

Mark 11:23

Truly, I say to you, whoever says to this mountain, 'Be taken up and thrown into the sea,' and does not doubt in his heart, but believes that what he expects will come to pass, it will be done for him.

Expectation is one of the secrets of success and is critical to materialization. First, we set our intention, and then we empower it with our expectation of it coming to pass. Without right expectation our future will remain rudimentary and not be fully realized.

Expectation is your God-given ability to make a demand on your future. That's a powerful statement. Your expectation (faith) connects you to the Laws of the Universe—the Law of Attraction, the Law of Correspondence, the Law of Manifestation and the Law of Mental Equivalents. Miracles—extraordinary things that happen to ordinary people—are delivered on the platform of expectation.

What do you expect God to do for you? Do you expect to have your way made plain and easy? Do you expect God to deliver on His promises to give you life more abundantly. Do you expect Divine Intervention when life's circumstances are not of your liking?

Expectancy is what moves God Energy. If you pray but never really expect God to answer your prayers, they won't be answered. You must pray from that place within you that knows and therefore expects that when you pray your prayers will be answered.

Joy is the emotion felt when one expects the best outcome to be evident. The joy of the successful journey is the joy that is apparent as one experiences the fulfillment of his expectations. Then there is the joy of completion. This is the joy of reflecting on one's life and recognizing all the expectations that were met over a lifetime.

Affirmation

Today I expect greater joy, more happiness, deeper peace and a more complete sense of Divine Power active in my life now. I dream more than others think is practical and expect more than most think is even possible.

Have a Little Faith

"Have faith in your own faith. The very smallest amount of faith (like a grain of mustard seed) is sufficient. It will build up more and more until the work is done." – EMMET FOX

I remember when my son Sharif was about fourteen years old. He was away at summer camp in the Pocono Mountains of Pennsylvania. One of the camper's confidence building activities was rock climbing. My son had no problem scaling the man-made mountain swiftly reaching the top. Once there, he realized that he had to come down. He looked down to steady his footing, only to have his glasses fall off his face and crash to the floor. His anxiety level catapulted to that of panic because of his extremely poor vision. He begged the camp counselor who was looking at him from below, to help him get down by some means other than climbing backwards all the while viewing the floor below and fearing that he might misstep and fall. Without his glasses he couldn›t see where he should place his feet. The counselor yelled up to him, "You've seen too much already. Don't look down, just have faith!" There was little else that he could do. The counselor wasn't coming to rescue him. He soon realized that anguishing over the climb down wasn't getting him to where he wanted to be, which was on solid ground. So he climbed down backwards, only looking upward until his feet solidly touched the floor.

Many of us are much the same way. We don't trust our own faith when we are challenged. When we undertake new activities, we don't realize that it is our faith that we are drawing upon. It never comes into question. It is when we meet with difficulty that our faith is put to the test. Jesus said,

"If ye have faith as a grain of mustard seed, ye shall say unto this mountain remove hence to yonder place, and it shall remove; and nothing shall be impossible unto you." Just a little faith carries us a long way. It has been said time and time again that the smallest amount of faith--the size of a mustard seed is sufficient.

In the Bible, Hebrews is full of instances proving faith's sustaining power. Paul enumerates the experiences of Moses, Noah, Abraham and Samuel as well as the prophets, whom through their faith subdued kingdoms, wrought righteousness, collected on God's promises, out of weakness were made strong and overcame their fears. Ernest Holmes, philosopher said, "If one will have faith in himself, faith in the Universe and in God, that faith will light the place in which he finds himself and by light of this faith, he will be able to see that all is good."

We are truly free from fear, worry and anxiety when we put our faith and trust in God whom we have not seen. Whoever prays has faith enough! I know from personal experience the freedom and relief I enjoy because I know that all is in God's mighty hands.

The implicit message in my son's story is that he looked only upward (God-ward) on his way down. Oh...how our lives would be transformed if only we kept our focus on God. Have faith in your own faith and grow it more and more by praying and trusting in God.

Affirmation:

I have faith in my own faith. I pray knowing that my faith is more than enough to move the mountains in my life.

Part IX

THE POWER
OF PRAYER

Prayer Is a Conduit to God

Prayer is constructive, because it enables us to establish closer contact
with the Fountain of Wisdom. Prayer is its own answer.
ERNEST HOLMES

Prayer is an act of invocation or request by means of thoughtful communication for the purpose of activating a rapport with God. As one type of spiritual practice, prayer can be either individual or communal, and may take place in public or in private. It may involve the use of words or song or may take the form of incantation. When we use language, prayer may be presented either as a formal doctrine or a spontaneous utterance by the person praying. Thanksgiving, worship, praise, as well as affirmative, and scientific prayer (also referred to as "spiritual mind treatment") are all different kinds of prayer. Spiritual mind treatments are performed for the purpose of changing for the better, our thoughts and perspectives about a condition or circumstance.

Whether expressed as a chant at a Tibetan monastery, a soulful rhythm at a Native American drumming circle, or a call to the Jewish Torah—all are forms of prayer. All forms draw us nearer to God. A moment of silence to honor the passing of a loved one or the muezzin calling from the minaret of a mosque are both expressions of prayer evoking our recognition of the Presence of the God Force to which each person who prays, prays.

Prayer is a recognized conduit to God. I believe that throughout our human journey most people pray, whether they call it prayer or something else. I believe that we are actually praying every time we ask for or think about needing help, guidance, direction, understanding, or strength within or outside of religion. If we pray without ceasing, our thoughts will always be in agreement with the Nature of God.

The human need to find an inner pathway to Spirit is as old as time itself. Even in these modern times, the longing to connect to something that transcends our worldly experience fosters the re-emergence of spirituality. Ralph Waldo Emerson described prayer from a practical perspective, i.e., "the contemplation of the facts of life from the highest point of view . . . the soliloquy of a beholding and jubilant sound. It is the Spirit of God pronouncing His good works." (*Essays, First Series: Essay II, Self-reliance*)

No matter the culture or the country, the religion or the philosophy, prayers are, for the most part, the same in intention—to connect to the Life Force, which is called by many names, including but not limited to Shiva, Buddha, Jehovah, Mother Nature, Great Spirit, God, the sunset, or the wind. Universally we long to connect with and talk to God, in the hope that we may be healed, supported, inspired, sustained, guided, or forgiven.

Prayer is a luminous, self-generating energy and a powerful act of honesty and humility. Usually, when we think to pray about a situation, it is because we have exhausted what we humanly know to do. When we pray in total and absolute surrender, our prayers are sincere, honest, and humble. Prayer is its own answer, offering the benefits of peace of mind, forgiveness of self and others, and opens us up to receive unconditional love. Prayer, like the sound of "OM" in solo or in a group, is a conduit to God.

Have you ever had a close, intimate and satisfying relationship with someone you never talked to? Of course you haven't, and it's absurd to even think it's possible. So why would you pretend to have a close relationship with God if you never pray? Prayer is important because it provides us with a way to offer God our gratitude, praise, and worship. Prayer helps us to realize our life in relation to God and works in both directions: when we talk to God, God speaks to us, revealing Itself through prayer – which is the conduit, if we listen and if we are receptive.

Often, when I don't know how to solve a problem or don't know how something is going to work out, I pray. I pray daily because it gives me confidence and hope and grows my trust in God, abolishing my fear and calming my uncertainty. Praying to God gives me solutions, ideas and, most of all, peace of mind.

Prayer is important because we need it. Let's be honest: God doesn't need our prayers as much as we need to pray. Invoking God's help has the power to change us, regardless of what we ask for. Prayer cultivates a dependency upon God; when we pray, we are asking for God's help or intervention. This act of surrender really takes the focus off ourselves and places it entirely upon God. It gives us a means to worship God, praise God, and thank God. Essentially, *prayer is our primary way of communicating with God*. In scripture, as in the Bible, God conveys His words to humanity. In prayer, humanity conveys our words to God.

Beyond the reasons already given, one of the main purposes for prayer is asking God to meet our daily needs. Prayer is a lifeline that humanity requires. With prayer we navigate and can change our world for the better.

Affirmation

Prayer connects me consciously with God-Mind. Through prayer, God is working to supply whatever I need. I accept the gift and give thanks for it even before it becomes apparent.

Divine Guidance Comes in Many Ways

"...With people this is impossible; with God all things are possible."
MATTHEW: 19:26

The days that followed one of the most disturbing times of my life were quiet and peaceful just like the calm after a storm. For about four months my world was turned upside down like a capsized boat slammed by forty-foot waves during a typhoon. I am referring to the wake that ensued when I declined a marriage proposal. To be someone's wife is the wish of most women young and old alike--mine too but under the right circumstances. In my mind, right circumstances simply involve being loved purely for oneself.

After four months of dating an undocumented immigrant, came the romantic, down-on-one-knee proposal of marriage. I never expected the reaction I got to the two-letter word 'no' in response to that unexpected premature question, "Will you marry me?" The dam burst right before my very eyes. Epithets infused with venom sprayed my way. Doors slammed as threats to my life and the lives of my children echoed from beyond.

The interesting thing about my reaction was that I was not afraid for myself, and with every atom of by being, I vowed to keep my children safe from the gale and out of harm's way.

It was simply amazing that I remained calm while being intimidated and spooked every day. I had just moved into a new development during the first phase of construction whereby my house was one of four on a block that stretched for half a mile. There were no houses on either side, no street lights—just the blackest, darkest skies and silence. On several nights my scorned suitor appeared from the shadows as I exited my car. He found the most secluded hiding places from which to jump out and threaten me and my children, all the while ranting, "You will marry me or I will haunt you to your death!"

He escalated his surprise appearances by showing up in Dallas, Los Angeles, and Atlanta while I was on business travel. He was a 'hacker" of sorts and accessed my computerized work calendar containing all the details of each trip—hotels, airlines and travel dates. He changed the phone message on my business line to one that impugned my professional reputation. I had all of my telephone numbers changed weekly to no avail. He would call me before they were even activated just to tease and annoy me.

The tipping point for me was when he showed up at my father's house threatening to kill him to make me feel guilty for "ruining his life." Had I been an atheist, I think I would have immediately become a believer in reaction to the guidance I was given that could only have come from God.

I was working in my office one day when the letters INS floated across my computer screen followed by the acronym FBI. The astonishing thing is that I was not searching the web for anything. The computer was just on. I was actually manually designing a course on a yellow legal pad and happened to look at the screen in thoughtful contemplation. Every day and every night I prayed for Divine Guidance to get out of that situation for good, always asking that the guidance come in ways that I could easily understand. The Immigration Naturalization Service (INS) made perfect sense to me, but the FBI left me clueless. By that time, I had hired a body guard to accompany me on my travels to New York where I worked often and where my stalker lived. Frank, my bodyguard, and I were chatting on the phone about my next trip, and I mentioned 'the miracle' and asked if he knew how the FBI fit into this scenario. As I recounted the recent scare tactics employed by my stalker, Frank yelled, "I've got it!" My telephone had been tampered, and the tampering constituted an FCC violation, a crime the FBI was responsible for addressing.

Several days after my return from the Empire State, I called the FBI. They asked me to come into the office. I went and recounted everything that had happened since I rejected the marriage proposal. Initially they were not convinced that this was anything more than a domestic dispute that should involve there agency. When I produced a check written for thousands of dollars that had been cashed, they began to take me seriously. While in New York and escorted by my bodyguard, I attempted to buy back my peace of mind by issuing my nemesis a check. That ploy only infuriated him more, and after cashing the check the telephone harassment resumed. I recorded all of his threats and took the recordings to the FBI. They had enough evidence to have him arrested by the INS. However, they released him after seventy-two hours because there was failed communication between the two agencies indicating that there was a pending case against him.

My nemesis, perturbed by my audacity to report him to the authorities, stole my car from my driveway and drove it back to New York. I reported the car stolen, and on one of his calls of tyranny I told him that "it was just a matter of time and he would again be arrested and this time for grand theft auto." After several days my car was found parked in the train station in Buffalo. I later learned that he had fled to Canada. I felt relieved and thought that I would finally have peace of mind again and my life restored to some sense of normalcy.

I savored the three weeks of the mundane routines of everyday life like cool waves of the ocean on my body on a scorching day. But the harassing calls resumed. Again, I recorded them and took them to the FBI. By this time they were invested in his deportation after being ridiculed for letting "a felonious, illegal alien slip through their fingers." I was coached by the FBI for several weeks on how to lure my harasser back to Maryland. We planned a 'sting' (a covert operation to apprehend a criminal) with me being a willing participant. That 007 stuff is really cool! After several weeks of pretending that I had had a change of heart and telling him that I was willing to marry him, he returned via Amtrak to Maryland for our reunion. As soon as he approached my car he was apprehended by the FBI. This time he was detained for two years before being deported back to Central America. In his mind, deportation back to poverty and a crime ridden country was a punishment worse than death.

It is true that time heals all, because after fourteen years I have forgiven him and he has forgiven me. He calls on my birthday and at Christmas reminiscing about the good times we had before his "psychotic episodes." He believes, as I do, that only the Power of God could have softened our hearts enough to forgive each other and leave the water under the bridge undisturbed.

As for me, I will always remember the power of prayer. I know that even when I don't know how to solve a problem, there is an Infinite Intelligence that does. All I have to do is look and listen for the ways in which I am divinely guided and then take action on that instruction. Praying brought me through this period of intense emotion. It calmed me and allowed me to surrender my challenges over to God. I found peace of mind through prayer and a long-term solution to my problem.

Affirmation:

In the stillness I ask for answers through my prayers. I listen for the voice from beyond. I heed the word of God and I find peace. All is right in my soul.

Part X

DOMINION

I Take Dominion over My Life

Most people do not really want freedom, because freedom involves
responsibility and most people are frightened of responsibility.
SIGMUND FREUD

To say that one takes dominion over his life is a bold statement and one
that comes with much responsibility. *Dominion* means to have authority
to rule, govern, or subdue. It also implies a self-governing territory. That
territory is your life.

Let me be clear that I am referring to spiritual dominion, which falls
under the auspices of God and is the outcome of aligning with the Will
of God. Taking dominion over our lives is knowing who we are—and
that we are created in the image and likeness of God regardless of what
we are experiencing in the world. God gave us a spirit of power, a spirit of
love, and a sound mind. Thus, we have within us the power to rise above
our circumstances.

Let us focus on the definition of dominion which also means to
subdue something. You see, when we operate in spiritual dominion, we
have the power and authority to subdue or oppress the enemy; the enemy
doesn't oppress us. The enemy of which I speak is any thought or outer
condition that precludes us from fully living life, such as fear, doubt,
worry, fact or circumstance.

God did not create slaves. He created sons and daughters who would
have dominion. Yet unless we are operating in dominion, we are slaves.
Whatever we don't have dominion over has dominion over us. For instance,
if we are worried about our finances, then money has dominion over us.

If we have an addiction, then our addiction has dominion over us. If we succumb to some physical condition, then that condition has dominion over us. We can't afford to be intimidated by what things appear to be, but rather we must rise up in the awareness of what God intends for us.

It would serve us well to be bold in our demands, as when we pray like Caleb, as written in the Bible in the book of Joshua. Caleb was an Israelite who came out of Egypt with his people and stood against the evil report of the spies. He wasn't affected by the opinions of the day or the circumstances that seemed out of control. Even when confronted with the possibility of death, he stood firm on God's promises and aligned with the Will of God. He proclaimed: "If the Lord delights in us, He will give us the land!" When Joshua announced the division of the land, Caleb stepped up and demanded with spiritual authority that he be given the mountain. "Give me what God said belongs to me. Give me my place of dominion. Give me my land, my space, my territory." He wasn't concerned about the challenges he would face or the battles that he would have to fight to govern his territory. Instead, he prayed for strength to face the challenges and planned strategies to win the battles. Thus, Caleb took dominion over his life and affairs.

How many times in our lives has the enemy tried to oppress us? Conditions and circumstances only have power over us when we forget our oneness with the Only Power and Presence there is—God, the Good, the Omnipotent. It is in our remembering that like Caleb, we too are ready to take dominion!

Affirmation

God is the only Power and Presence in my life. Conditions have no power over me. Personalities have no power over me. I take dominion.

Sacred Service: My Utmost for God

Sacred service is not something that occupies only a portion of our lives.
It is not limited to just one activity or a certain number of activities.
It takes in every aspect of our daily living.
WATCHTOWER

Sacred means to be devoted or dedicated to a deity. *Service* is an act of helpful activity.

In that beautiful devotional song, "I Give Myself Away," the lyrics read:

"I give myself away,
So that you (God) can use me.
Here I am . . . here I stand.
Lord, my life is in your hands."

What those lyrics are expressing is that anything we do out of pure motive for our Creator and in service to God and humanity is sacred service and the highest form of worship. It goes on to say: "Lord, I long to see your desires revealed in me."

The way that God's desires are revealed through us is through sacred service. When we are keepers of our brothers and sisters...when we are selfless in our actions and in caring for others, we serve the Higher Good. We are saying "Yes" to Life and the Universe when we are in service to others.

"My life is not my own.
To Spirit I belong.
I give myself away." (in service.)

Answering the call to be God's hands, mouth, and feet on earth is not for the faint of heart because it demands unwavering commitment. Indeed it requires our utmost for the glory of our Creator.

Ernest Holmes believed that service is the keynote to success and implies constructive work and loyalty to Spirit. Constructive work is anything that uplifts others, aids others, or makes better any given situation or circumstance. Holmes said, "As practitioners (all who practice spiritual mind treatment and the Science of Mind philosophy), sacred service is not something that occupies only a portion of our lives." It is not limited to just one activity or a certain number of activities but is present in every aspect of our daily living.

In Foundations class, an introductory course to the Science of Mind philosophy, "Sacred Service" is presented as a spiritual practice. And what is a practice? It is something that we do with repetition and consistency. It becomes an integral part of our lives. Most of us pronounce the word service as "serve us." And the truth of the matter is that being in service to others really does serve us. Just think about it: Have you ever been in a situation when life hit you hard? Or, when the stars didn't align with the solar system called your life?

When I have those kinds of experiences, I immediately find a way to be in "service" to others. Why? The benefits to me are tremendous. For one, I forget about my problems; and oftentimes when I am helping those less fortunate than myself I am reminded of just how abundantly blessed I am. You see, service does serve us.

At a difficult time in my life—the passing of my husband—I was completing my Practitioner studies. My ministry, if you will, was to develop and offer a bereavement support program to my spiritual community. We didn't have a pastoral care ministry at the time. Providing bereavement support to others served me well. It took my mind off the reality of my own life. It served me by giving me another example of how those who are servants to others are in fact served by their own actions. The servants become the beneficiaries.

We can learn about service to others from the Hindus: *Seva* means volunteer work, selfless service, work offered to God and, literally, *in the service of man lies the service of God.* One must not forget that if one serves the sick, the poor, or any other person in distress, one would be offering prayers to God in the highest form. A very important concept in Hinduism is *dharma*. It means correct action, and in accordance with *dharma, seva is* also understood as service to humanity and to God and the right thing to do. Thus sacred service means being of service to others to the highest or greatest degree of one's own ability.

Affirmation

I serve others and am therefore served, blessed and healed by my own actions.

Affirmations

Work

Every negative thought or condition is erased from my experience. I walk in the joy of expectancy of ever-increasing good in the form of my right income generating opportunities and the manifestation of my dreams. I accept my good right now.

Money

Money and prosperity come to me through my consciousness. I do not allow fear and feelings of unworthiness to occupy space in my mind. I confidently remain open to the flow of ideas that come to me and I create new realities by acting on these ideas. I am grateful for the unlimited possibilities of the Divine flowing as money and prosperity into my life now. And so it is!

Success

Success is mine! Failure is not an option. I persistently pursue my goals and dreams until they are realized. The doorway of my consciousness has the word SUCCESS written boldly above it. I am confident in my ability to succeed in all I attempt with earnest desire.

Perseverance

I do not drown in my problems. They have no power over me. I face them head on. I allow myself to feel whatever emotions that surface. And when I have done all that I can do, I just stand and let the living waters of Spirit guide, nurture and heal me.

I glorify the vision in my mind of having a wonderful life. My idea of my perfect life is enthroned in my heart. I imagine it, I breathe it. I make the most of what I have, applying what I know to live the life of my dreams.

Change

There is a time for everything, and a season for every activity under the heavens. ---- Ecclesiastes 3:1

Today, I declare that each time I change my mind I change my experience. I declare that life is an eternal adventure of greater and better experiences.

Gratitude

I am grateful for everything I experience in this lifetime. With gratitude as a way of life I vibrate at high levels, attracting corresponding experiences into my life. Amen, Amen my life is a blessed life. Amen, Amen my life is blessed.

Grace, Love & Forgiveness

I serve and am served by the gifts I have to give—the gifts given to me by the life I am privileged to live. My faith comes from the certainty of God's Grace.

I freely bestow the gift of love to others without exception or expectation but love always returns to me pressed down and running over.

When I forgive, grace is present. When I listen, grace is present. When I aid another, grace is present. The Grace of God is upon me always.

As I follow the path of forgiveness, I set my past free and forgive myself for my participation in holding resentments. As my heart opens, I am free to give and receive love.

Self-Inquiry

Today I uncover the perfection within me. I look upon the world of my affairs knowing that the Spirit within makes my way immediate and easy. I know there is nothing in me that could possibly obstruct or withhold the Divine Circuit of Life, Success, and Prosperity from me. Light casts out all shadows.

Faith

I have faith in my own faith. I pray knowing that my faith is more than enough to move the mountains in my life.

Freedom

Today I manifest freedom. I have the freedom to enjoy living. I am free to love and be loved. I am free to give full expression to every capacity I possess.

Intention

I sincerely believe that the Laws of God are Good and Perfect and these laws are manifesting as my experience now! I believe that the nature of my thought externalizes itself to bring about conditions that correspond exactly to where I place my attention. I am grateful for the happiness, the joy, the health, the wealth, and the right people that have been attracted to me. I am in complete acceptance of that which I have designed as my life now. I let it be so.

Prayer

I am the change I wish to see in the world. I know that prayer is a powerful force for good and is my conduit to God. I pray because I know it changes me. I face every situation with faith and confidence since my prayers are answered even before I ask.

In the stillness I ask for answers through my prayers. I listen for the voice from beyond. I heed the word of God and I find peace. All is right in my life.

In the stillness I ask for answers through my prayers. I listen for the voice from beyond. I heed the word of God and I find peace. All is right in my soul.

Dominion

God is the only Power and Presence in my life. Conditions have no power over me. Personalities have no power over me. I take dominion.

Service

I serve others and am therefore served and healed by my own actions.

Meet the Author

As a public speaker, consultant, and visionary for over thirty years, Michele K. Synegal has delivered inspirational talks, workshops, and seminars that have made her one of the esteemed teachers in the field of leadership and personal development. For more than three decades she has served as president of Management Dynamics, Inc., a national company providing consulting services to Fortune 100 companies and government agencies in the area of workforce optimization, leadership development, diversity, inclusion, and equity.

Michele is the creator World Day of Service within Centers for Spiritual Living wherein its ministries around the globe serve the less fortunate in the communities where they live and work. For ten years she has served as a spiritual leader within that international movement, as chair and member of its Minister Council and in her own spiritual community, Spiritual Empowerment Center in Baltimore, MD. As a highly sought after inspirational speaker, life coach, and minister, Michele has empowered individuals to be their personal best and to achieve new levels of spiritual awareness and personal success.

She holds a Master's Degree in Consciousness Studies from the Holmes Institute, a premiere graduate school that prepares spiritual, transformational leaders. Her undergraduate studies were in Human Relations and Organizational Behavior at the University of San Francisco. The two most significant accomplishments of her life are her children, Briana and Sharif Mitchell.

List of Works Consulted

Castaneda, Carlos. *The Active Side of Infinity*. New York: Harper Perennial, 1999.

Dyer, Wayne. *The Power of Intention*. Carlsbad, CA: Hay House, 2005.

Emerson, Ralph Waldo. *Essays, First Series: Essay II, Self-reliance*. New York: Gramercy Publishing, 1993.

Hawkins, Dr. David. *Power vs Force*. West Sedona, AZ: Veritas Publishing, 2013.

Holmes, Ernest. *The Science of Mind*. New York: Penguin Books, 1998.

This Thing Called Life. New York: Tarcher Publishing, 2007.

LaFollette, Hugh. *International Encyclopedia of Ethics*. Hoboken, NJ: Wiley-Blackwell, 2013.

Mandela Prison Archive. Houghton, South Africa: Nelson Mandela Foundation, 1977.

May, Gerald C. *The Awakened Heart: Opening Yourself to the Love You Need*. New York: HarperOne, 1993.

Weldes, Reverend Petra, and Reverend Christian Sorensen. *The Joyous Living Journal*. Golden CO: Spiritual Living Press, 2009.

Printed in the United States
By Bookmasters